LEVEL II SCHWESER'S SECRET SAUCE®

D1449425

SCHWESER'S SECRET SAUCE®: 2016 LEVEL II CFA®

©2016 Kaplan, Inc. All rights reserved.

Published in 2016 by Kaplan Schweser.

Printed in the United States of America.

ISBN: 978-1-4754-3632-7

PPN: 3200-7006

FOREWORD

Secret Sauce® is a valuable addition to the study tools of any CFA exam candidate. It offers concise and readable explanations of the major parts of the Level II CFA curriculum.

This book does not cover every Learning Outcome Statement (LOS) and, as you are aware, any LOS is "fair game" for the exam. We focus here on those LOS that are core concepts in finance and accounting, have application to other LOS, are complex and difficult for candidates, or require memorization of characteristics or relationships.

Secret Sauce is easy to carry with you and will allow you to study these key concepts, definitions, and techniques over and over, an important part of mastering the material. When you get to topics where the coverage here appears too brief or raises questions in your mind, this is your cue to go back to your study notes to fill in the gaps in your understanding. There is no shortcut to learning the very broad array of subject matter covered by the Level II curriculum, but this volume should be a valuable tool for learning and reviewing the material as you progress in your studies over the months leading up to exam day.

Pass rates remain around 45%, and returning Level II candidates make comments such as, "I was surprised at how difficult the exam was." You should not despair because of this, but you should also not underestimate this challenge. Our study materials, practice exams, question bank, videos, seminars, and Secret Sauce are all designed to help you study as efficiently as possible, grasp and retain the material, and apply it with confidence on exam day.

Best regards,

Bijesh Tolia

Dr. Bijesh Tolia, CFA, CA
Vice President of CFA Education
and Level II Manager
Kaplan Schweser

Kent Westlund

Kent Westlund, CFA
Content Specialist

Ethical and Professional Standards

Topic Weight on Exam	10–15%
SchweserNotes™ Reference	Book 1, Pages 1–110

For many candidates, ethics is difficult material to master. Even though you are an ethical person, you will not be prepared to perform well on this portion of the Level II exam without a comprehensive knowledge of the Standards of Professional Conduct.

Up to 15% of Level II exam points come from the ethics material, so you should view this topic as an area where you can set yourself apart from the person sitting next to you in the exam room. CFA Institute has indicated that performance on the ethics material serves as a "tie-breaker" for exam scores very close to the minimum passing score. This is referred to as the "ethics adjustment."

What's the point? *The ethics material is worth taking seriously.* With 10–15% of the points and the possibility of pushing a marginal exam into the pass column (not to mention the fact that as a candidate you are obligated to abide by CFA Institute Standards), it is foolhardy not to devote substantial time to Level II ethics.

A Study Plan for Ethics

The big question is, "What do I need to know?" The answer is that you really need to be able to apply all of the ethics material. You simply must spend time learning the Standards and developing some intuition about how CFA Institute expects you to respond on the exam. Here are several quick guidelines to help in your preparation:

- *Focus on the Standards.* The Standards of Professional Conduct are the key to the ethics material. The Code of Ethics is a poetic statement of objectives, but the heart of the testing comes from the Standards.

- *Broad interpretation.* A broad definition of most standards is needed for testing purposes *even if it seems too broad to apply in your "real world" situation.* For instance, a key component of the professional standards is the concept of disclosure (e.g., disclosure of conflicts of interest, compensation plans, and soft dollar arrangements). On the exam, you need to interpret what needs to be disclosed very broadly. A good guideline is that if there is any question in your mind about whether a particular bit of information needs to be disclosed, then it most certainly needs disclosing. *Err on the side of massive disclosure!*
- *Always side with the employer.* Many view the Code and Standards to be an employer-oriented document. That is, for many readers the employer's interests seem to be more amply protected. If there is a potential conflict between the employee and employer, always side with the employer.
- *Defend the charter.* CFA Institute views itself as the guardian of the industry's reputation and, specifically, the guardian of the CFA® designation. On the exam, be very suspicious of activity that makes industry professionals and CFA charterholders look bad.
- *Assume all investors are inexperienced.* Many different scenarios can show up on the exam (e.g., a money manager contemplating a trade for a large trust fund). However, when you study this material, view the Standards from the perspective of a money manager with fiduciary responsibility for a small account belonging to inexperienced investors. Assuming that the investors are inexperienced makes some issues more clear.

Now, how should you approach this material? There are two keys here.

- *First, you need to read the material very carefully.* We suggest that you underline key words and concepts and commit them to memory. It's probably a good idea to start your study effort with a careful read of ethics and then go over the material again in May.
- *Second, you should answer every practice ethics question you can get your hands on to develop some intuition.* The truth is that on the exam, you are going to encounter a number of ethics questions that you don't immediately know the answer to. Answering a lot of practice questions will help you develop some intuition about how CFA Institute expects you to interpret the ethical situations on the exam. Also, study every example in the *Standards of Practice Handbook* and be prepared for questions on the exam that test similar concepts.

THE CODE OF ETHICS
Cross-Reference to CFA Institute Assigned Topic Review #1

Members of the CFA Institute and candidates for the CFA designation must:

- Act with integrity, competence, diligence, and respect, and in an ethical manner with the public, clients, prospective clients, employers, employees, colleagues in the investment profession, and other participants in the global capital markets.

- Place the integrity of the investment profession and the interests of clients above their own personal interests.
- Use reasonable care and exercise independent professional judgment when conducting investment analysis, making investment recommendations, taking investment actions, and engaging in other professional activities.
- Practice and encourage others to practice in a professional and ethical manner that will reflect credit on themselves and the profession.
- Promote the integrity and viability of the global capital markets for the ultimate benefit of society.
- Maintain and improve their professional competence and strive to maintain and improve the competence of other investment professionals.

STANDARDS OF PROFESSIONAL CONDUCT
Cross-Reference to CFA Institute Assigned Topic Review #2

The following is a summary of the Standards of Professional Conduct. Focus on the purpose of the standard, applications of the standard, and proper procedures of compliance for each standard.

Standard I: Professionalism

I(A) **Knowledge of the Law.** Understand and comply with laws, rules, regulations, and Code and Standards of any authority governing your activities. In the event of a conflict, follow the more strict law, rule, or regulation. Do not knowingly participate or assist in violations, and dissociate from any known violation.

> *Professor's Note: The requirement to disassociate from any violations committed by others is explicit in the Standard. This might mean resigning from the firm in extreme cases. The guidance statement also makes clear that you aren't required to report potential violations of the Code and Standards committed by other members or candidates to CFA Institute, although it is encouraged. Compliance with any applicable fiduciary duties to clients would now be covered under this standard.*

I(B) **Independence and Objectivity.** Use reasonable care to exercise independence and objectivity in professional activities. Don't offer, solicit, or accept any gift, benefit, compensation, or consideration that would compromise either your own or someone else's independence and objectivity.

Professor's Note: The prohibition against accepting gifts, benefits, compensation, or other consideration that might compromise your independence and objectivity includes all situations beyond just those involving clients and prospects, including investment banking relationships, public companies the analyst is following, pressure on sell-side analysts by buy-side clients, and issuer-paid research.

I(C) **Misrepresentation.** Do not knowingly misrepresent facts regarding investment analysis, recommendations, actions, or other professional activities.

Professor's Note: Plagiarism is addressed under the broader category of misrepresentation.

I(D) **Misconduct.** Do not engage in any professional conduct that involves dishonesty, fraud, or deceit. Do not do anything that reflects poorly on your integrity, good reputation, trustworthiness, or professional competence.

Professor's Note: The scope of this standard addresses only professional misconduct and not personal misconduct. There is no attempt to overreach or regulate one's personal behavior.

Standard II: Integrity of Capital Markets

II(A) **Material Nonpublic Information.** If you are in possession of nonpublic information that could affect an investment's value, do not act or induce someone else to act on the information.

Professor's Note: This Standard addressing insider trading states that members and candidates must not act or cause others to act on material nonpublic information until that same information is made public. This is a strict standard—it does not matter whether the information is obtained in breach of a duty, is misappropriated, or relates to a tender offer. The "mosaic theory" still applies, and an analyst can take action based on her analysis of public and nonmaterial nonpublic information.

II(B) **Market Manipulation.** Do not engage in any practices intended to mislead market participants through distorted prices or artificially inflated trading volume.

Standard III: Duties to Clients

III(A) **Loyalty, Prudence, and Care.** Always act for the benefit of clients and place clients' interests before your employer's or your own interests. You must be loyal to clients, use reasonable care, and exercise prudent judgment.

Professor's Note: Applicability of any fiduciary duties to clients and prospects is now covered under Standard I(A) Knowledge of the Law.

III(B)　**Fair Dealing**. You must deal fairly and objectively with all clients and prospects when providing investment analysis, making investment recommendations, taking investment action, or in other professional activities.

Professor's Note: This Standard includes providing investment analysis and engaging in other professional activities as well as disseminating investment recommendations and taking investment action.

III(C)　**Suitability**
1.　When in an advisory relationship with a client or prospect, you must:
- Make reasonable inquiry into a client's investment experience, risk and return objectives, and constraints prior to making any recommendations or taking investment action. Reassess information and update regularly.
- Be sure investments are suitable to a client's financial situation and consistent with client objectives before making recommendations or taking investment action.
- Make sure investments are suitable in the context of a client's total portfolio.
2.　When managing a portfolio, your investment recommendations and actions must be consistent with the stated portfolio objectives and constraints.

Professor's Note: The client's written objectives and constraints are required to be reviewed and updated "regularly." The second item applies the suitability standard to managed portfolios and requires you to stick to the mandated investment style as outlined in the portfolio objectives and constraints.

III(D)　**Performance Presentation**. Presentations of investment performance information must be fair, accurate, and complete.

III(E)　**Preservation of Confidentiality**. All information about current and former clients and prospects must be kept confidential unless it pertains to illegal activities, disclosure is required by law, or the client or prospect gives permission for the information to be disclosed.

Professor's Note: This Standard covers all client information, not just information concerning matters within the scope of the relationship. Also note that the language specifically includes not only prospects but former clients. Confidentiality regarding employer information is covered in Standard IV.

Standard IV: Duties to Employers

IV(A)   **Loyalty.** You must place your employer's interest before your own and must not deprive your employer of your skills and abilities, divulge confidential information, or otherwise harm your employer.

Professor's Note: The phrase "in matters related to employment" means that you are not required to subordinate important personal and family obligations to your job. The Standard also addresses the issue of "whistle-blowing" by stating that there are circumstances in which the employer's interests are subordinated to actions necessary to protect the integrity of the capital markets or client interests.

IV(B)   **Additional Compensation Arrangements.** No gifts, benefits, compensation, or consideration that may create a conflict of interest with the employer's interest are to be accepted, unless written consent is received from all parties.

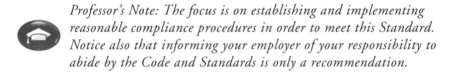

Professor's Note: "Compensation" includes "gifts, benefits, compensation, or consideration."

IV(C)   **Responsibilities of Supervisors.** You must make reasonable efforts to ensure that anyone subject to their supervision or authority complies with applicable laws, rules, regulations, and the Code and Standards.

Professor's Note: The focus is on establishing and implementing reasonable compliance procedures in order to meet this Standard. Notice also that informing your employer of your responsibility to abide by the Code and Standards is only a recommendation.

Standard V: Investment Analysis, Recommendations, and Actions

V(A)   **Diligence and Reasonable Basis**

1.   When analyzing investments, making recommendations, and taking investment actions, use diligence, independence, and thoroughness.

2.   Investment analysis, recommendations, and actions should have a reasonable and adequate basis, supported by research and investigation.

Professor's Note: This Standard explicitly requires that you exercise diligence and have a reasonable basis for investment analysis, as well as for making recommendations or taking investment action.

V(B)   **Communication With Clients and Prospective Clients**

1. Disclose to clients and prospects the basic format and general principles of investment processes they use to analyze and select securities and construct portfolios. Promptly disclose any process changes.

2. Disclose to clients and prospective clients significant limitations and risks associated with the investment process.

3. Use reasonable judgment in identifying relevant factors important to investment analyses, recommendations, or actions, and include those factors when communicating with clients and prospects.

4. Investment analyses and recommendations should clearly differentiate facts from opinions.

 Professor's Note: This Standard covers communication in any form with clients and prospective clients, including research reports and recommendations.

V(C)   **Record Retention**. Maintain all records supporting analysis, recommendations, actions, and all other investment-related communications with clients and prospects.

 Professor's Note: The issue of record retention is a separate Standard, emphasizing its importance. It includes records relating to investment analysis as well as investment recommendations and actions. The guidance statement says you should maintain records for seven years in the absence of other regulatory guidance.

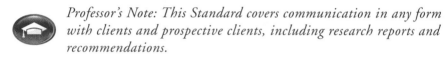

Standard VI: Conflicts of Interest

VI(A)   **Disclosure of Conflicts**. You must make full and fair disclosure of all matters that may impair your independence or objectivity or interfere with your duties to employer, clients, and prospects. Disclosures must be prominent, in plain language, and effectively communicate the information.

 Professor's Note: The emphasis is on meaningful disclosure in prominent and plain language; impenetrable legal prose that no one can understand is not sufficient.

VI(B)   **Priority of Transactions**. Investment transactions for clients and employers must have priority over those in which you are a beneficial owner.

 Professor's Note: The language is intended to be clear—transactions for clients and employers always have priority over personal transactions.

VI(C)   **Referral Fees.** You must disclose to your employers, clients, and prospects any compensation, consideration, or benefit received by, or paid to, others for recommendations of products and services.

Standard VII: Responsibilities as a CFA Institute Member or CFA Candidate

---

VII(A)   **Conduct as Participants in CFA Institute Programs.** You must not engage in conduct that compromises the reputation or integrity of CFA Institute, the CFA designation, or the integrity, validity, or security of CFA Institute programs.

> *Professor's Note: The Standard is intended to cover conduct such as cheating on the CFA exam or otherwise violating rules of CFA Institute or the CFA program. It is not intended to prevent anyone from expressing any opinions or beliefs concerning CFA Institute or the CFA program. Violations also include discussing the questions (or even broad subject areas) that were tested or not tested on the exam.*

VII(B)   **Reference to CFA Institute, the CFA Designation, and the CFA Program.** You must not misrepresent or exaggerate the meaning or implications of membership in CFA Institute, holding the CFA designation, or candidacy in the program.

> *Professor's Note: This Standard prohibits you from engaging in any conduct that may "misrepresent or exaggerate the meaning or implications of membership in CFA Institute, holding the CFA designation, or candidacy in the CFA program." You cannot reference any "partial" designation, since this also misrepresents or exaggerates credentials.*

OTHER LEVEL II ETHICS TOPIC REVIEWS

The Code and Standards are the heart of the Level II ethics curriculum, so we recommend spending about 80% of your ethics study time on them. However, some additional ethics topic reviews at Level II may be tested, including the CFA Institute Research Objectivity Standards. Spend the other 20% of your time on these topics and focus on the key points discussed in the following sections. Remember that the Research Objectivity Standards are applicable only to firms (as opposed to individuals) who claim compliance.

CFA Institute Research Objectivity Standards
Cross-Reference to CFA Institute Assigned Topic Review #3

The Research Objectivity Standards are voluntary standards intended to complement and facilitate compliance with the Standards of Practice. They are intended to be a universal guide for all investment firms by providing ethical standards and practices regarding full and fair disclosure of any conflicts or potential conflicts relating to the firm's research and investment recommendations. However, firms are not required to comply with the Research Objectivity Standards.

Professor's Note: If you have an understanding of the basic requirements, you should be able to handle most of the questions on the topic that might appear on the Level II exam. We also suggest that you review the Recommended Procedures for Compliance.

Figure 1: Key Requirements of the CFA Institute Research Objectivity Standards

Category	Key Requirements
Research Objectivity Policy	• Have a formal, written policy and distribute it to clients, prospective clients, and employees. • Senior office must attest annually that firm complies with policy.
Public Appearances	• Disclose conflicts of interest when discussing research and recommendations in public forums.
Reasonable and Adequate Basis	• All reports and recommendations must have a reasonable and adequate basis.
Investment Banking	• Separate research analysts from investment banking. • Don't let analysts report to, or be supervised by, investment banking personnel. • Don't let investment banking review, revise, or approve research reports and recommendations.
Research Analyst Compensation	• Link analyst compensation to quality of analysis, not amount of investment banking business done with client.
Relationships With Subject Companies	• Don't let subject companies see issue rating or recommendation prior to release, or promise a specific rating or recommendation.
Personal Investments and Trading	• Don't engage in front running of client trades. • Don't let employees and immediate family members trade ahead of clients, trade contrary to firm recommendations, or participate in IPOs of companies covered by the firm.
Timeliness of Research Reports and Recommendations	• Issue research reports on a timely basis.
Compliance and Enforcement	• Enforce policies and compliance procedures, assess disciplinary sanctions, monitor effectiveness of procedures, and maintain records.
Disclosure	• Disclose conflicts of interest.
Rating System	• Have a rating system that investors find useful and provide them with information they can use to determine suitability.

QUANTITATIVE METHODS

Topic Weight on Exam	5–10%
SchweserNotes™ Reference	Book 1, Pages 111–245

Quantitative analysis is one of the primary tools used in the investment community, so you can expect CFA Institute to test this section thoroughly. Both linear regression (with only one independent variable) and multiple regression (with more than one independent variable) are covered in the Level II Quant readings. The Level II curriculum also includes a topic review on time series analysis.

A key topic in the Level II Quant material is multiple regression. If you have a solid understanding of simple linear regression, you can handle multiple regression and anything you might see on the Level II exam. All the important concepts in simple linear regression are repeated in the context of multiple regression (e.g., testing regression parameters and calculating predicted values of the dependent variable), and you're most likely to see these tested as part of a multiple regression question.

For the time series material, the concepts of nonstationarity, unit roots (i.e., random walks), and serial correlation, will be important, as well as being able to calculate the mean-reverting level of an autoregressive (AR) time-series model. Understand the implications of seasonality and how to detect and correct it, as well as the root mean squared error (RMSE) as a model evaluation criterion.

CORRELATION AND REGRESSION
Cross-Reference to CFA Institute Assigned Topic Review #9

Because everything you learn for simple linear regression can be applied to multiple linear regression, you should focus on the material presented in the next section. The only topics unique to simple linear regression are (1) the correlation coefficient, (2) regression assumptions, and (3) forming a prediction interval for the dependent (Y) variable.

Correlation Coefficient

The *correlation coefficient, r,* for a sample and ρ for a population, is a measure of the strength of the linear relationship (correlation) between two variables. A correlation coefficient with a value of +1 indicates that two variables move exactly together

---

(perfect positive correlation), a value of −1 indicates that the variables move exactly opposite (perfect negative correlation), and a value of 0 indicates no linear relationship.

The test statistic for the significance of a correlation coefficient (null is $\rho = 0$) has a t-distribution with $n - 2$ degrees of freedom and is calculated as:

$$t = \frac{r\sqrt{n-2}}{\sqrt{1-r^2}}$$

Regression Assumptions

- A *linear relationship* exists between the dependent and independent variables.
- The *independent variable is uncorrelated with the residual term*.
- The expected value of the *residual term is zero*.
- There is a *constant variance* of the residual term.
- The *residual term is independently distributed*; that is, the residual term for one observation is not correlated with that of another observation (a violation of this assumption is called autocorrelation).
- The *residual term is normally distributed*.

Note that five of the six assumptions are related to the residual term. The residual terms are independently (of each other and the independent variable), identically, and normally distributed with a zero mean.

Confidence Interval for a Predicted Y-Value

In simple linear regression, you have to know how to *calculate a confidence interval for the predicted Y value:*

predicted Y value ± (critical t-value)(standard error of forecast)

Calculating a confidence interval for the predicted *y* value is *not* part of the multiple regression LOS, however, because the multiple regression version is too complicated and not part of the Level II curriculum.

MULTIPLE REGRESSION AND ISSUES IN REGRESSION ANALYSIS
Cross-Reference to CFA Institute Assigned Topic Review #10

Multiple regression is the most important part of the quant material. You can fully expect that multiple regression will be on the exam, probably in several places.

The flow chart in Figure 1 will help you evaluate a multiple regression model and grasp the "big picture" in preparation for the exam.

Figure 1: Assessment of a Multiple Regression Model

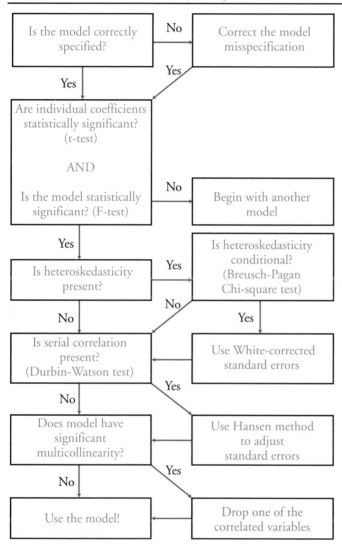

You should know that a *t*-test assesses the statistical significance of the individual regression parameters, and an *F*-test assesses the effectiveness of the model as a whole in explaining the dependent variable. You should understand the effect that heteroskedasticity, serial correlation, and multicollinearity have on regression results. *Focus on interpretation of the regression equation and the test statistics.*

A regression of a dependent variable (e.g., sales) on three independent variables would yield an equation like the following:

$$Y_i = b_0 + (b_1 \times X_{1i}) + (b_2 \times X_{2i}) + (b_3 \times X_{3i}) + \varepsilon_i$$

You should be able to interpret a multiple regression equation, test the slope coefficients for statistical significance, and use an estimated equation to forecast (predict) the value of the dependent variable. Remember, when you are forecasting a value for the dependent variable, you use estimated values for all the independent variables, even those independent variables whose slope coefficient is not statistically different from zero.

Multiple Regression: Testing

Tests for significance in multiple regression involve testing whether:

- Each independent variable *individually* contributes to explaining the variation in the dependent variable using the *t*-statistic.
- Some or all of the independent variables contribute to explaining the variation in the dependent variable using the *F*-statistic.

Tests for individual coefficients. We conduct hypothesis testing on the estimated slope coefficients to determine if the independent variables make a significant contribution to explaining the variation in the dependent variable. With multiple regression, *the critical* t-*stat is distributed with n – k – 1 degrees of freedom*, where *n* is the number of observations and *k* is the number of independent variables.

$$t = \frac{\text{estimated regression parameter}}{\text{standard error of regression parameter}} \text{ with } n - k - 1 \text{ df}$$

ANOVA is a statistical procedure that attributes the variation in the dependent variable to one of two sources: the regression model or the residuals (i.e., the error term). The structure of an ANOVA table is shown in Figure 2.

©2016 Kaplan, Inc.

Figure 2: Analysis of Variance (ANOVA) Table

Source	df (Degrees of Freedom)	SS (Sum of Squares)	MS (Mean Square = SS/df)
Regression	k	RSS	$MSR = \dfrac{RSS}{k}$
Error	$n - k - 1$	SSE	$MSE = \dfrac{SSE}{n - k - 1}$
Total	$n - 1$	SST	

Note that RSS + SSE = SST. The information in an ANOVA table can be used to calculate R^2, the F-statistics, and the standard error of estimate (SEE).

The *coefficient of determination* (R^2) is the percentage of the variation in the dependent variable explained by the independent variables.

$$R^2 = \frac{\text{regression sum of squares (RSS)}}{\text{total sum of squares (SST)}}$$

$$= \frac{\text{SST} - \text{sum of squared errors (SSE)}}{\text{SST}}$$

In multiple regression, you also need to understand *adjusted R^2*. The adjusted R^2 provides a measure of the goodness of fit that adjusts for the number of independent variables included in the model.

The *standard error of estimate* (SEE) measures the uncertainty of the values of the dependent variable around the regression line. It is approximately equal to the standard deviation of the residuals. If the relationship between the dependent and independent variables is very strong, the SEE will be low.

$$\text{standard error of estimate (SEE)} = \sqrt{\text{mean squared error (MSE)}}$$

Tests of all coefficients collectively. For this test, the null hypothesis is that all the slope coefficients simultaneously equal zero. The required test is a one-tailed F-test and the calculated statistic is:

$$F = \frac{\text{regression mean square (MSR)}}{\text{mean squared error (MSE)}} \text{ with k and } n - k - 1 \text{ df}$$

The F-statistic has two distinct degrees of freedom, one associated with the numerator (k, the number of independent variables) and one associated with the denominator ($n - k - 1$). The critical value is taken from an F-table. The decision rule for the *F*-test is reject H_0 if F > $F_{critical}$. *Remember that this is always a one-tailed test.*

Rejection of the null hypothesis at a stated level of significance indicates that at least one of the coefficients is significantly different than zero, which is interpreted to mean that at least one of the independent variables in the regression model makes a significant contribution to the explanation of the dependent variable.

Confidence Intervals

The confidence interval for a regression coefficient in a multiple regression is calculated and interpreted exactly the same as with a simple linear regression:

regression coefficient ± (critical t-value)(standard error of regression coefficient)

If zero is contained in the confidence interval constructed for a coefficient at a desired significance level, we conclude that the slope is not statistically different from zero.

Potential Problems in Regression Analysis

You should be familiar with the three violations of the assumptions of multiple regression and their effects.

Figure 3: Problems in Regression Analysis

	Conditional Heteroskedasticity	*Serial Correlation*	*Multicollinearity*
What is it?	Residual variance related to level of independent variables	Residuals are correlated	Two or more independent variables are correlated
Effect?	Too many Type I errors	Type I errors (for positive correlation)	Too many Type II errors

Model Misspecification

There are six common misspecifications of the regression model that you should be aware of and be able to recognize:

1. Omitting a variable.
2. Transforming variable.

©2016 Kaplan, Inc.

3. Incorrectly pooling data.
4. Using a lagged dependent variable as an independent variable.
5. Forecasting the past.
6. Measuring independent variables with error.

The effects of the model misspecification on the regression results are basically the same for all the misspecifications: regression coefficients are biased and inconsistent, which means we can't have any confidence in our hypothesis tests of the coefficients or in the predictions of the model.

TIME-SERIES ANALYSIS
Cross-Reference to CFA Institute Assigned Topic Review #11

Types of Time Series

Linear Trend Model

The typical time series uses time as the independent variable to estimate the value of time series (the dependent variable) in period t:

$$y_t = b_0 + b_1(t) + \varepsilon_t$$

The predicted change in y is b_1 and t = 1, 2, ..., T

Trend models are limited in that they assume time explains the dependent variable. Also, they tend to be plagued by various assumption violations. The Durbin-Watson test statistic can be used to check for serial correlation. A linear trend model may be appropriate if the data points seem to be equally distributed above and below the line and the mean is constant. Growth in GDP and inflation levels are likely candidates for linear models.

Log-Linear Trend Model

Log-linear regression assumes the dependent financial variable grows at some constant rate:

$$y_t = e^{b_0 + b_1(t)}$$

$$\ln(y_t) = \ln(e^{b_0 + b_1(t)}) \Rightarrow \ln(y_t) = b_0 + b_1(t)$$

The log-linear model is best for a data series that exhibits a trend or for which the residuals are correlated or predictable or the mean is non-constant. Most of the data related to investments have some type of trend and thus lend themselves more to a log-linear model. In addition, any data that have seasonality are candidates for a log-linear model. Recall that any exponential growth data call for a log-linear model.

The use of the transformed data produces a linear trend line with a better fit for the data and increases the predictive ability of the model. Because the log-linear model more accurately captures the behavior of the time series, the impact of serial correlation in the error terms is minimized.

Autoregressive (AR) Model

In AR models, the dependent variable is regressed against previous values of itself.

An autoregressive model of order p can be represented as:

$$x_t = b_0 + b_1 x_{t-1} + b_2 x_{t-2} + \dots + b_p x_{t-p} + \varepsilon_t$$

There is no longer a distinction between the dependent and independent variables (i.e., x is the only variable). An AR(p) model is specified correctly if the autocorrelations of residuals from the model are not statistically significant at any lag.

When testing for serial correlation in an AR model, don't use the Durbin-Watson statistic. Use a t-test to determine whether any of the correlations between residuals at any lag are statistically significant.

If some are significant, the model is incorrectly specified and a lagged variable at the indicated lag should be added.

Chain Rule of Forecasting

Multiperiod forecasting with AR models is done one period at a time, where risk increases with each successive forecast because it is based on previously forecasted values. The calculation of successive forecasts in this manner is referred to as the *chain rule of forecasting*. A one-period-ahead forecast for an AR(1) model is determined in the following manner:

$$\hat{x}_{t+1} = \hat{b}_0 + \hat{b}_1 x_t$$

Likewise, a 2-step-ahead forecast for an AR(1) model is calculated as:

$$\hat{x}_{t+2} = \hat{b}_0 + \hat{b}_1 \hat{x}_{t+1}$$

Autocorrelations

One of the assumptions underlying linear regression is that the residuals are uncorrelated with each other. If a time series model's residuals exhibit serial correlation, the model is not appropriate for the time series and we should not use it to predict future performance without making appropriate corrections.

Covariance Stationary

Statistical inferences based on a lagged time series model may be invalid unless we can make the assumption that the time series being modeled is covariance stationary. A time series is covariance stationary if it satisfies the following three conditions:

1. Constant and finite expected value.
2. Constant and finite variance.
3. Constant and finite covariance with leading or lagged values.

To determine whether a time series is covariance stationary, we can:

- Plot the data to see if the mean and variance remain constant (often detects seasonality).
- Run an AR model and test correlations.
- Perform the Dickey-Fuller test (which is a test for a unit root, or if $b_1 - 1$ is equal to zero).

If the times series does not satisfy these conditions, we say it is not covariance stationary, or that there is nonstationarity. Most economic and financial time series relationships are not stationary. The degree of nonstationarity depends on the length of the series and the underlying economic and market environment and conditions.

For an AR(1) model to be covariance stationary, the mean reverting level must be defined. Stated differently, b_1 must be less than one.

If the AR model is not covariance stationary, we can often correct it with first differencing.

Mean Reversion

A time series is mean reverting if it tends towards its mean over time. The mean reverting level for an AR(1) model is $\dfrac{b_0}{(1-b_1)}$.

The value of the dependent variable tends to fall when above its mean and rise when below its mean.

Unit Root

If the value of the lag coefficient is equal to one, the time series is said to have a unit root and will follow a random walk process. A series with a unit root is not covariance stationary. Economic and finance time series frequently have unit roots. First differencing will often eliminate the unit root. If there is a unit root, this period's value is equal to last period's value plus a random error term and the mean reverting level is undefined.

Random Walk

A random walk time series is one for which the value in one period is equal to the value in another period, plus a random (unpredictable) error. If we believe a time series is a random walk (i.e., has a unit root), we can transform the data to a covariance stationary time series using a procedure called first differencing.

Random walk without a drift: $x_t = x_{t-1} + \varepsilon_t$

Random walk with a drift: $x_t = b_0 + x_{t-1} + \varepsilon_t$

- In either case, the mean reverting level is undefined ($b_1 = 1$), so the series is not covariance stationary.
- Need to use first differencing, and the new dependent variable is the change in x from one period to the next.

First Differencing

The first differencing process involves subtracting the value of the time series (i.e., the dependent variable) in the immediately preceding period from the current value of the time series to define a new dependent variable, y. If the original time series has a unit root, this means we can define y_t as:

$$y_t = x_t - x_{t-1} \Rightarrow y_t = \varepsilon_t$$

Then, stating *y* in the form of an AR(1) model:

$$y_t = b_0 + b_1 y_{t-1} + \varepsilon_t$$

where:
$$b_0 = b_1 = 0$$

This transformed time series has a finite mean-reverting level of $\dfrac{0}{1-0} = 0$ and is, therefore, covariance stationary.

First differencing can remove a trend in the data and result in a covariance stationary series.

Professor's Note: By taking first differences, you model the change in the value of the dependent variable rather than the value of the dependent variable.

Seasonality

Seasonality in a time series is tested by calculating the autocorrelations of error terms. A statistically significant lagged error term may indicate seasonality. To adjust for seasonality in an AR model, an additional lag of the independent variable (corresponding to the statistically significant lagged error term) is added to the original model. Usually, if quarterly data are used, the seasonal lag is 4; if monthly data are used, the seasonal lag is 12. If a seasonal lag coefficient is appropriate and corrects the seasonality, a revised model incorporating the seasonal lag will show no statistical significance of the lagged error terms.

Assessing Forecast Accuracy With Root Mean Squared Error (RMSE)

Root mean squared error (RMSE) is used to assess the predictive accuracy of autoregressive models. For example, you could compare the results of an AR(1) and an AR(2) model. The RMSE is the square root of the average (or mean) squared error. The model with the lower RMSE is better.

Out-of-sample forecasts predict values using a model for periods beyond the time series used to estimate the model. The RMSE of a model's out-of-sample forecasts should be used to compare the accuracy of alternative models.

Structural Change (Coefficient Instability)

Estimated regression coefficients change from one time period to another. There is a trade off between the statistical reliability of a long time series and the stability of a short time series. You need to ask, has the economic process or environment changed?

A structural change is indicated by a significant shift in the plotted data at a point in time that seems to divide the data into two distinct patterns. When this is the case, you have to run two different models, one incorporating the data before and one after that date, and test whether the time series has actually shifted. If the time series has shifted significantly, a single time series encompassing the entire period (i.e., both patterns) will likely produce unreliable results, so the most recent model may be more appropriate.

Cointegration

Cointegration means that two time series are economically linked (related to the same macro variables) or follow the same trend and that relationship is not expected to change. If two time series are cointegrated, the error term from regressing one on the other is covariance stationary and the *t*-tests are reliable.

To test whether two time series are cointegrated, we regress one variable on the other using the following model:

$$y_t = b_0 + b_1 x_t + \varepsilon$$

where:
y_t = value of time series y at time t
x_t = value of time series x at time t

The residuals are tested for a unit root using the Dickey-Fuller test with critical *t*-values calculated by Engle and Granger (i.e., the DF-EG test). If the test *rejects* the null hypothesis of a unit root, we say the error terms generated by the two time series are covariance stationary and the two series are cointegrated. If the two series are cointegrated, we can use the regression to model their relationship.

Occasionally, an analyst will run a regression using two time series (i.e., two time series with different variables). For example, to use the market model to estimate the equity beta for a stock, the analyst regresses a time series of the stock's returns on a time series of returns for the market.

- If both time series are covariance stationary, model is reliable.
- If only the dependent variable time series or only the independent time series is covariance stationary, the model is not reliable.
- If neither time series is covariance stationary, you need to check for cointegration.

Autoregressive Conditional Heteroskedasticity (ARCH)

ARCH describes the condition where the variance of the residuals in one time period within a time series is dependent on the variance of the residuals in another period. When this condition exists, the standard errors of the regression coefficients in AR models and the hypothesis tests of these coefficients are invalid.

The ARCH(1) regression model is expressed as:

$$\hat{\varepsilon}_t^2 = a_0 + a_1 \hat{\varepsilon}_{t-1}^2 + \mu_t$$

If the coefficient, a_1, is statistically different from zero, the time series is ARCH(1).

If a time-series model has been determined to contain ARCH errors, regression procedures that correct for heteroskedasticity, such as generalized least squares, must be used in order to develop a predictive model. Otherwise, the standard errors of the model's coefficients will be incorrect, leading to invalid conclusions.

However, if a time series has ARCH errors, an ARCH model can be used to predict the variance of the residuals in following periods. For example, if the data exhibit an ARCH(1) pattern, the ARCH(1) model can be used in period t to predict the variance of the residuals in period t + 1:

$$\hat{\sigma}_{t+1}^2 = \hat{a}_0 + \hat{a}_1 \hat{\varepsilon}_t^2$$

Summary: The Time-Series Analysis Process

The following steps provide a summary of the time-series analysis process. Note that you may not need to go through all nine steps. For example, notice that by Step C, if there is no seasonality or structural change and the residuals do not exhibit serial correlation, the model is appropriate.

Step A: Evaluate the investment situation you are analyzing and select a model. If you choose a time series model, follow steps B through I.

Step B: Plot the data and check that it is covariance stationarity. Signs of nonstationarity include linear trend, exponential trends, seasonality, or a structural change in the data.

Step C: If no seasonality or structural change, decide between a linear or log-linear model.
  • Calculate the residuals.
  • Check for serial correlation using the Durbin-Watson statistic.
  • If no serial correlation, model is appropriate to use.

Step D: If you find serial correlation, prepare to use an auto regressive (AR) model by making it covariance stationary. This includes:
  • Correcting for a linear trend—use first differencing.
  • Correcting for an exponential trend—take natural log and first difference.
  • Correcting for a structural shift—estimate the models before and after the change.
  • Correcting for seasonality—add a seasonal lag (see Step G).

Step E: After the series is covariance stationary, use an AR(1) model to model the data.
  • Test residuals for significant serial correlations.
  • If no significant correlation, model is okay to use.

Step F: If the residuals from the AR(1) exhibit serial correlation, use an AR(2) model.
  • Test residuals for significant serial correlations.
  • If no significant correlation, model is okay to use.
  • If significant correlation found, keep adding to the AR model until there is no significant serial correlation.

Step G: Check for seasonality.
  • Plot data.
  • Check seasonal residuals (autocorrelations) for significance.
  • If residuals are significant, add the appropriate lag (e.g., for monthly data, add the 12th lag of the time series).

Step H: Check for ARCH.

Step I: Test the model on out-of-sample data.

PROBABILISTIC APPROACHES: SCENARIO ANALYSIS, DECISION TREES, AND SIMULATIONS
Cross-Reference to CFA Institute Assigned Topic Review #12

Steps in Running a Simulation:

1. Determine the probabilistic variables.

2. Define probability distributions for these variables.

3. Check for correlations among variables.

4. Run the simulation.

Three Ways to Define the Probability Distributions for a Simulation's Variables

There are three bases to defining the probability distributions for a simulation's variables:

1. historical data,

2. cross-sectional data, or

3. rely on the analyst's subjective estimation of the appropriate distribution.

How to Treat Correlation Across Variables in a Simulation

When there is a strong correlation between variables used in a simulation, we can either

1. allow only one variable to vary and algorithmically compute the other variable, or

2. build the correlation behavior into the simulation.

Advantages of Using Simulations in Decision Making:

1. The analyst is encouraged to more carefully estimate the inputs.

2. The expected-value output takes the form of a distribution of expected value and thus is more informative than a point estimate.

Issues in Using Simulations in Risk Assessment:

1. Input data quality.

2. Inappropriate specification of statistical distributions.

3. Non-stationary distributions.

4. Non-stationary (dynamic) correlations.

Care should be taken to not double count risk: double-counting happens when we simultaneously adjust the discount rate for risk and also apply a penalty for the variability in value.

Figure 4: Comparison of Scenario Analysis, Decision Trees, and Simulations

Appropriate Method	Distribution of Risk	Sequential?	Accomodates Correlated Variables?
Simulations	Continuous	Does not matter	Yes
Scenario analysis	Discrete	No	Yes
Decision trees	Discrete	Yes	No

Economics

Topic Weight on Exam	5–10%
SchweserNotes™ Reference	Book 1, Pages 246–326

Economics will most likely be tested by asking you to apply the investment tools you learn in this section to the analysis of equity, fixed income, and derivative securities. For example, the lessons learned from economic growth models can be applied to the credit analysis of sovereign debt in Study Session 14. As you read through the Level II economics material, look for links to security valuation and think about how the concepts might be tested as part of a broader valuation item set.

CURRENCY EXCHANGE RATES: DETERMINATION AND FORECASTING

Cross-Reference to CFA Institute Assigned Topic Review #13

Currency Cross Rates

A *cross rate* is the rate of exchange between two currencies implied by their exchange rates with a common third currency.

Suppose we are given three currencies A, B, and C. We can have three pairs of currencies (i.e., A/B, A/C, and B/C).

Rules:

$$\left(\frac{A}{C}\right)_{bid} = \left(\frac{A}{B}\right)_{bid} \times \left(\frac{B}{C}\right)_{bid}$$

$$\left(\frac{A}{C}\right)_{offer} = \left(\frac{A}{B}\right)_{offer} \times \left(\frac{B}{C}\right)_{offer}$$

To calculate the profits from a *triangular arbitrage*, imagine that three currencies each represent a corner of a triangle. Begin with a first currency (usually given in the question—we call it the home currency) and go around the triangle by exchanging the home currency for the first foreign currency, then exchanging the first foreign currency for the second foreign currency, and then exchanging the

---

second foreign currency back into the home currency. If we end up with more money than we started with, we've earned an arbitrage profit.

The bid-ask spread forces us to buy a currency at a higher rate going one way than we can sell it for going the other way.

Follow the "up-the-bid-and-multiply and down-the-ask-and-divide" rule.

Example: Triangular arbitrage

The following quotes are available from your dealer.

Quotes:
USD/EUR 1.271–1.272
EUR/GBP 1.249–1.250
USD/GBP 1.600–1.601

Is an arbitrage profit possible? If so, compute the arbitrage profit in USD if you start with USD 1 million.

Answer:

The implied cross rates:

$$\left(\frac{USD}{GBP}\right)_{bid} = \left(\frac{USD}{EUR}\right)_{bid} \times \left(\frac{EUR}{GBP}\right)_{bid} = 1.271 \times 1.249 = 1.587$$

$$\left(\frac{USD}{GBP}\right)_{ask} = \left(\frac{USD}{EUR}\right)_{ask} \times \left(\frac{EUR}{GBP}\right)_{ask} = 1.272 \times 1.250 = 1.590$$

Since the dealer quote of USD/GBP = 1.600–1.601 falls outside of these cross rates, arbitrage profit may be possible (i.e., we have to check it).

There are two possible paths around the triangle (we are given the starting position in USD):

Path 1: USD → GBP → EUR → USD

Path 2: USD → EUR → GBP → USD

Since the dealer quotes imply that USD is undervalued relative to GBP (it costs more in USD to buy GBP using the dealer quote compared to the implied cross rates), if arbitrage exists, it will be via path 2. Make sure to use dealer quotes in the steps below instead of implied cross rates.

Step 1: Convert 1 million USD into EUR @ 1.272 = EUR 786,164
Step 2: Convert EUR 786,164 into GBP @ 1.250 = GBP 628,931
Step 3: Convert GBP 628,931 into USD @ 1.600 = USD 1,006,289

Arbitrage profit = USD 6,289

Note: In step 1, we are going from USD to EUR ("down" the USD/EUR quote), hence we divide USD 1,000,000 by the ask rate of 1.272. The same logic is used for steps 2 and 3. Note also that we did not have to compute the implied cross rate to solve this problem: we could've simply computed the end result using both paths to see if either would give us an arbitrage profit.

Mark-to-Market Value of a Forward Contract

The *mark-to-market value* of a forward contract reflects the profit that would be realized by closing out the position at current market prices, which is equivalent to offsetting the contract with an equal and opposite forward position:

$$V_t = \frac{(FP_t - FP)(\text{contract size})}{\left[1 + R\left(\dfrac{\text{days}}{360}\right)\right]}$$

where:

V_t = value of the forward contract at time t (to the party buying the base currency), denominated in the price currency.

FP_t = forward price (to sell base currency) at time t in the market for a new contract maturing at time T ($t < T$).

days = number of days remaining to maturity of the forward contract (T–t).

R = the interest rate of the price currency.

Example: Mark-to-market value of a forward contract

Yew Mun Yip has entered into a 90-day forward contract long CAD 1 million against AUD at a forward rate of 1.05358 AUD/CAD. Thirty days after initiation, the following AUD/CAD quotes are available:

Maturity	FX Rate
Spot	1.0612/1.0614
30-day	+4.9/+5.2
60-day	+8.6/+9.0
90-day	+14.6/+16.8
180-day	+42.3/+48.3

The following information is available (at t=30) for AUD interest rates:

30-day rate: 1.12%

60-day rate: 1.16%

90-day rate: 1.20%

What is the mark-to-market value in AUD of Yip's forward contract?

©2016 Kaplan, Inc.

Answer:

Yip's contract calls for long CAD (i.e., converting AUD to CAD). To value the contract, we would look to unwind the position. To unwind the position, Yip can take an offsetting position in a new forward contract with the same maturity. Hence, Yip would be selling CAD in exchange for AUD and, hence, going up the bid (i.e., use the bid price). Note that after 30 days, 60 more days remain in the original contract.

The forward bid price for a new contract expiring in T – t = 60 days is 1.0612 + 8.6/10,000 = 1.06206.

The interest rate to use for discounting the value is also the 60-day AUD interest rate of 1.16%:

$$V_t = \frac{(FP_t - FP)(\text{contract size})}{\left[1 + R\left(\dfrac{\text{days}}{360}\right)\right]} = \frac{(1.06206 - 1.05358)(1,000,000)}{\left[1 + 0.0116\left(\dfrac{60}{360}\right)\right]} = 8,463.64$$

Thirty days into the forward contract, Yip's position has gained (positive value) AUD 8,463.64. This is because Yip's position is long CAD, which has appreciated relative to AUD since inception of the contract. Yip can close out the contract on that day and receive AUD 8,463.64.

Note: Be sure to use the AUD (price currency) interest rate.

International Parity Conditions

Note: Exchange rates (where applicable) below follow the convention of A/B.

Covered interest arbitrage:

Covered interest rate parity holds when any forward premium or discount exactly offsets differences in interest rates so an investor would earn the same return investing in either currency. Covered in this context means it holds by arbitrage.

$$F = \frac{\left(1 + R_A\left(\dfrac{\text{days}}{360}\right)\right)}{\left(1 + R_B\left(\dfrac{\text{days}}{360}\right)\right)} S_0$$

Uncovered interest rate parity:

Uncovered interest rate parity relates expected future spot exchange rates (instead of forward exchange rates) to interest rate differentials. Since the expected spot price is not market traded, uncovered interest rate parity does not hold by arbitrage.

$$E(\%\Delta S)_{(A/B)} = R_A - R_B$$

Comparing covered and uncovered interest parity, we see that covered interest rate parity gives us the no-arbitrage forward exchange rate, while uncovered interest rate parity concerns changes in the *expected* future spot exchange rate (which is not market traded).

International Fisher relation:

$$R_A - R_B = E(\text{inflation}_A) - E(\text{inflation}_B)$$

This relation tells us that the difference between two countries' nominal interest rates should be approximately equal to the difference between their expected inflation rates.

Relative purchasing power parity (relative PPP) states that changes in exchange rates should exactly offset the price effects of any inflation differential between two countries.

Relative PPP:

$$\%\Delta S_{(A/B)} = \text{inflation}_{(A)} - \text{inflation}_{(B)}$$

Figure 1: The International Parity Relationships Combined

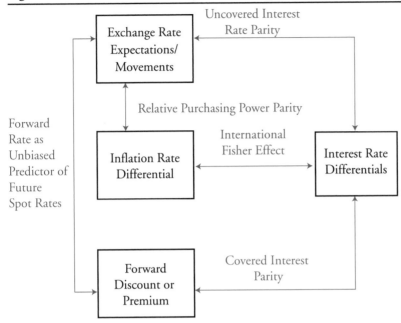

Several observations can be made from the relationships among the various parity relationships:

- Covered interest parity holds by arbitrage. If forward rates are unbiased predictors of future spot rates, uncovered interest rate parity also holds (and vice versa).
- Interest rate differentials should mirror inflation differentials. This holds true if the international Fisher relation holds. If that is true, we can also use inflation differentials to forecast future exchange rates which is the premise of the ex-ante version of PPP.
- If the ex-ante version of relative PPP as well as the international Fisher relation both hold, uncovered interest rate parity will also hold.

Real Exchange Rates

If relative PPP holds at any point in time, the *real exchange rate* will be constant, and is called the equilibrium real exchange rate. However, since relative PPP seldom holds over the short term, the real exchange rate fluctuates around this mean-reverting equilibrium value.

$$\text{real exchange rate (A/B)} = \text{equilibrium real exchange rate}$$
$$+ (\text{real interest rate}_B - \text{real interest rate}_A)$$
$$- (\text{risk premium}_B - \text{risk premium}_A)$$

Several observations can be made about the relationship identified above:

- This relationship should only be used to assess the direction of change (i.e., appreciate/depreciate) in real exchange rates rather than precise estimates of exchange rates.
- In the short term, the real value of a currency fluctuates around its long-term, equilibrium value.
- The real value of a currency is positively related to its real interest rate and negatively related to the risk premium investors demand for investing in assets denominated in the currency.
- The real interest rate increases when the nominal interest rate increases (keeping inflation expectations unchanged) or when expected inflation decreases (keeping nominal interest rates unchanged).

Taylor Rule

The Taylor rule links the central bank's policy rate to economic conditions (employment level and inflation) and can be used to forecast exchange rates. Under the Taylor rule, the real interest rate is positively related to both inflation gap and output gap.

$$\text{real interest rate} = r = r_n + \alpha(\pi - \pi^*) + \beta(y - y^*)$$

where:
r = Taylor rule implied real policy interest rate
r_n = Neutral *real* policy interest rate
π = Current inflation rate
π^* = Central bank's target inflation rate
y = log of current level of output
y^* = log of central bank's target (sustainable) output
α, β = policy response coefficients (>0; Taylor suggested a value of 0.5 for both)

The Taylor rule advises that the policy rate should be raised in response to positive inflation and output gaps.

Because exchange rates are positively related to the real interest rate in a country (due to capital inflows to countries with high real interest rates), exchange rates should also be positively related to inflation gaps and output gaps.

The FX Carry Trade

The *FX carry trade* seeks to profit from the failure of uncovered interest rate parity to hold in the short run. In an FX carry trade, the investor invests in a high-yield currency while borrowing in a low-yield currency. If the higher yield currency does not depreciate by the interest rate differential, the investor makes a profit.

> profit on carry trade
> = interest differential – change in the spot rate of investment currency

The carry trade is inherently a leveraged trade that is exposed to crash risk, as the underlying return distributions of carry trades are non-normal (negative skewness and excess kurtosis). Risk management in carry trade may be implemented through a valuation filter or a volatility filter.

Balance of Payments (BOP) Analysis

BOP influence on exchange rates can be analyzed based on current account influence and capital account influence.

Current account influences include:

- *Flow mechanism*: A current account deficit puts downward pressure on the exchange value of a country's currency. The decrease in the value of the currency *may* restore the current account deficit to a balance depending on the initial deficit, the influence of exchange rates on export and import prices, and the price elasticity of demand of traded goods.
- *Portfolio composition mechanism*: Investor countries with capital account deficits (and current account surpluses) may find their portfolios dominated by investments in countries persistently running capital account surpluses (and current account deficits). If/when the investor countries rebalance their portfolios, the investee countries' currencies may depreciate.
- *Debt sustainability mechanism*: A country running a current account deficit may be running a capital account surplus by borrowing from abroad. When the level of debt gets too high relative to GDP, investors may question the sustainability of this level of debt, leading to a rapid depreciation of the borrower's currency.

Capital account inflows (outflows) are one of the major causes of appreciation (depreciation) of a country's currency.

Approaches to Exchange Rate Determination

1. Mundell-Fleming model

Figure 2 shows the impact of monetary and fiscal policies in the short run under the *Mundell-Fleming model*.

Figure 2: Monetary and Fiscal Policy and Exchange Rates

Monetary Policy/Fiscal Policy	*Capital Mobility*	
	High	*Low*
Expansionary/expansionary	Uncertain	Depreciation
Expansionary/restrictive	Depreciation	Uncertain
Restrictive/expansionary	Appreciation	Uncertain
Restrictive/restrictive	Uncertain	Appreciation

2. **Monetary models**

The monetary models focus on the influence of monetary policy on inflation and, hence, exchange rates.

  A) **Pure monetary model:** PPP holds at any point in time and, therefore, an expansionary monetary policy results in an increase in inflation and a depreciation of the home currency.

  B) **Dornbusch overshooting model:** A restrictive (expansionary) monetary policy leads to an appreciation (depreciation) of the domestic currency in the short term and then a slow depreciation (appreciation) toward the long-term PPP value.

3. **Portfolio balance model (asset market approach):** Focuses on the long-term implications of sustained fiscal policy (deficit or surplus) on currency values. When the government runs a fiscal deficit, it borrows money from investors. Under the portfolio balance approach, sustained fiscal deficits will lead to eventual depreciation of the home currency.

Capital Controls and Central Bank Intervention

Capital controls and central bank intervention aim to reduce excessive capital inflows which could lead to speculative bubbles. The success of central bank intervention depends on the size of official FX reserves at the disposal of the central bank relative to the average trading volume in the country's currency. For developed markets, central bank resources on a relative basis are too insignificant to be effective at managing exchange rates. However, some emerging market countries with large FX reserves relative to trading volume have been somewhat effective. Persistent and large capital flows are harder for central banks to manage using capital controls.

Warning Signs of an Impending Currency Crisis

- Terms of trade deteriorate.
- Official foreign exchange reserves dramatically decline.
- Real exchange rate is substantially higher than the mean-reverting level.
- Inflation increases.
- Equity markets experience a boom-bust cycle.
- Money supply relative to bank reserves increases.
- Nominal private credit grows.

ECONOMIC GROWTH AND THE INVESTMENT DECISION
Cross-Reference to CFA Institute Assigned Topic Review #14

Preconditions for Economic Growth

The following factors are positively related to growth rate of an economy:

- Level of savings and investment.
- Developed financial markets and intermediaries.
- Political stability, rule of law, and property rights.
- Investment in human capital (e.g., education, health care).
- Favorable tax and regulatory systems.
- Free trade and unrestricted capital flows.

Sustainable Growth Rate of an Economy

In the long run, the rate of aggregate stock market appreciation is limited to the sustainable growth rate of the economy.

Potential GDP

Potential GDP represents the maximum output of an economy without putting upward pressure on prices. Higher potential GDP growth increases the potential for stock returns and also increases the credit quality of fixed income investments.

In the short term, the difference between potential GDP and actual GDP may be useful for predicting fiscal/monetary policy. If actual GDP is less than potential GDP, inflation is unlikely and the government may follow an expansionary policy.

Capital Deepening Investment and Technological Process

Cobb-Douglas Production Function

$$Y = TK^{\alpha}L^{(1-\alpha)}$$

where:

Y	= the level of aggregate output in the economy
α and $(1-\alpha)$	= the share of output allocated to capital (K) and labor (L), respectively
T	= a scale factor that represents the technological progress of the economy, often referred to as *total factor productivity* (TFP)

The *Cobb-Douglas function* essentially states that output (GDP) is a function of labor and capital inputs, and their productivity. It exhibits constant returns to scale; increasing all inputs by a fixed percentage leads to the same percentage increase in output.

Dividing both sides by L in the Cobb-Douglas production function, we can obtain the output per worker (labor productivity).

$$\text{output per worker} = Y/L = T(K/L)^{\alpha}$$

Capital deepening is an increase in the capital stock and the capital-to-labor ratio. Due to diminishing marginal product of capital, increases in the capital stock can lead to only limited increases in output and labor productivity if the capital-to-labor ratio is already high.

Technological progress impacts the productivity of all inputs—labor and capital. The long-term growth rate can be increased by technological progress (also called *total factor productivity*) since output and labor efficiency are increased at all levels of capital-to-labor ratios.

In steady state (i.e., equilibrium), the marginal product of capital (MPK = $\alpha Y/K$) and marginal cost of capital (i.e., the *rental price of capital*, r) are equal, hence $\alpha Y/K = r$.

The productivity curves in Figure 3 show the effect of increasing capital per worker on output per worker. Capital deepening is a movement *along* the productivity curve. The curvature of the relationship derives from the diminishing marginal productivity of capital. Technological progress *shifts* the productivity curve upward and will lead to increased productivity at all levels of capital per worker.

Figure 3: Productivity Curves

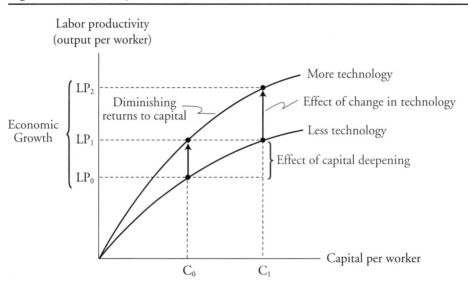

Growth Accounting Relations

growth rate in potential GDP = long-term growth rate of technology +
α (long-term growth rate in capital) +
$(1-\alpha)$ (long-term growth rate in labor)

or

growth rate in potential GDP = long-term growth rate of labor force +
long-term growth rate in labor productivity

> **Example: Estimating potential GDP growth rate**
>
> Azikland is an emerging market economy where labor accounts for 60% of total factor cost. The long-term trend of labor growth of 1.5% is expected to continue. Capital investment has been growing at 3%. The country has benefited greatly from borrowing the technology of more developed countries; total factor productivity is expected to increase by 2% annually. **Compute** the potential GDP growth rate for Azikland.
>
> **Answer:**
>
> Using the growth accounting equation,
>
> $$\%\Delta Y = 2\% + (0.4)(3\%) + (0.6)(1.5\%) = 4.1\%$$

Theories of Economic Growth

Classical growth theory contends that growth in real GDP per capita is temporary—when the GDP per capita rises above the subsistence level, a population explosion occurs and GDP per capita is driven back to the subsistence level.

Neoclassical growth theory contends that the sustainable growth rate of an economy is a function of population growth, labor's share of income, and the rate of technological advancement. Growth gains from other means, such as increased savings, are only temporary.

Under the neoclassical growth theory, *sustainable growth of output per capita* (g^*) is equal to growth rate in technology (θ) divided by labor's share of GDP ($1-\alpha$):

$$g^* = \frac{\theta}{(1-\alpha)}$$

The sustainable growth rate of output (G^*) is equal to the sustainable growth rate of output per capita plus growth of labor (ΔL).

Neoclassical theory yields several implications about sustainable growth and inputs:

- Capital deepening affects the level of output but not the growth rate in the long run. Capital deepening may lead to temporary growth but growth will revert back to the sustainable level if there is no change in technology.
- The growth rate in an economy will move toward its steady state rate regardless of initial capital to labor ratio or level of technology.
- In the long term, the growth rate in productivity (i.e., output per capita) is a function of only the growth rate of technology (θ) and the share of labor to total output ($1-\alpha$).
- An increase in savings will only temporarily raise the rate of growth in an economy. However, countries with a higher savings rate will enjoy a higher capital to labor ratio and higher productivity.

Endogenous growth theory acknowledges the impact of technological progress within the model. Under endogenous growth theory, investment in capital can have constant returns, unlike neoclassical theory which assumes diminishing returns to capital. This assumption allows for a permanent increase in growth rate attributable to an increase in savings rate. Research and development expenditures are often cited as examples of capital investment that increase technological progress.

Convergence Hypotheses

The **absolute convergence** hypothesis states that less-developed countries will converge to the standard of living of developed countries.

The **conditional convergence** hypothesis assumes that convergence in living standards will occur for countries with the same savings rate, population growth, and production functions.

The **club convergence** hypothesis contends that some less developed countries may converge to developed standards if they are in the "club" of countries. A club comprises countries with similar institutional structures, such as property rights and political stability. Countries outside of the club (without the appropriate institutional structures) will not converge.

ECONOMICS OF REGULATION
Cross-Reference to CFA Institute Assigned Topic Review #15

Regulations and Regulators

Regulations can be classified as:

- *Statutes* (laws made by legislative bodies).
- *Administrative regulations* (rules issued by government agencies or other bodies authorized by the government).
- *Judicial law* (findings of courts).

Regulators can be government agencies or independent regulators. *Independent regulators* can either be *self-regulatory organizations* (SROs) or non-SROs. Additionally, there are *outside bodies* like FASB that are not regulators themselves, but their output (standards in the case of FASB) are referenced by regulators.

Figure 4: Type of Regulators

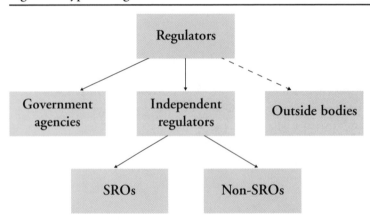

SROs without government recognition are not considered regulators. Self-regulating organizations, while independent of the government and relatively immune from political pressure, may still be subject to pressure from their members. Independent SROs—when properly supervised by regulatory agencies—have been effective in carrying out the objectives of the regulation.

Economic Rationale for Regulation

Regulations are needed in the presence of:

- *Informational frictions*, when information is not equally available or distributed.
- *Externalities*, which deal with the consumption of public goods wherein cost is not proportional to consumption.

Regulatory Interdependencies

The **regulatory capture** theory states that a regulatory body will eventually be influenced or even controlled by the industry that is it is supposed to regulate. Regulatory differences between jurisdictions can lead to *regulatory competition* wherein regulators compete to provide the most attractive regulatory environment. Firms may take advantage of **regulatory arbitrage** to exploit the difference between the substance and interpretation of a regulation or the differences between regulations in different countries.

Regulatory Tools

Tools of regulatory intervention include price mechanisms (taxes or subsidies), restrictions on or requirement of certain activities (e.g., banning use of certain chemicals or requiring the filing of financial reports), the provision of public goods (such as roads), and financing of private projects (e.g., funding organizations that are beneficial to society).

Cost/Benefit Analysis of Regulations

Regulatory burden refers to the cost of compliance for the entity being regulated. Regulatory burden minus the private benefits of regulation is known as the *net regulatory burden*. Indirect costs of regulations need to be included in the cost-benefit analysis, but are difficult to measure ex-ante. *Sunset clauses* require a cost-benefit analysis to be revisited before the associated regulation is renewed.

FINANCIAL REPORTING AND ANALYSIS

Topic Weight on Exam	15–20%
SchweserNotes™ Reference	Book 2, Pages 10–220

INVENTORY COST FLOW METHOD

Cross-Reference to CFA Institute Assigned Topic Review #16

The choice of inventory cost flow method (known as the cost flow assumption under U.S. GAAP and cost formula under IFRS) affects the firm's income statement, balance sheet, and many financial ratios. Additionally, the cost flow method can affect the firm's income taxes and, thus, the firm's cash flow. Cost of goods sold (COGS) is related to the beginning balance of inventory, purchases, and the ending balance of inventory.

COGS = beginning inventory + purchases – ending inventory

Notice that the COGS and ending inventory are inversely related. In other words, if a particular valuation method increases the value of ending inventory, the COGS would be lower under that method.

Inventory cost flow methods:

1. FIFO: The cost of the first item purchased is the cost of the first item sold. Ending inventory is based on the cost of the most recent purchases, thereby approximating current cost.

2. LIFO: The cost of the last item purchased is the cost of the first item sold. Ending inventory is based on the cost of the earliest items purchased. Assuming inflation, ending inventory is smaller and COGS is larger compared to those calculated using FIFO. Higher COGS results in lower taxes and, thus, higher cash flow. LIFO is prohibited under IFRS.

3. Weighted average cost: COGS and inventory values are between their FIFO and LIFO values.

4. Specific identification: Each unit sold is matched with the unit's actual cost.

©2016 Kaplan, Inc.

LIFO Reserve

The LIFO reserve is the difference in LIFO ending inventory and FIFO ending inventory. It is used to adjust the LIFO firm's ending inventory and COGS back to FIFO for comparison purposes. To adjust a LIFO firm's financial statements to reflect the FIFO cost flow method:

1. Add the LIFO reserve to current assets (ending inventory).

2. Subtract the income taxes on the LIFO reserve from current assets (cash).

3. Add the LIFO reserve, net of tax, to shareholders' equity.

4. Subtract the *change* in the LIFO reserve from COGS.

5. Add the income taxes on the *change* in the LIFO reserve to income tax expense.

LIFO Liquidation

A LIFO liquidation occurs when a firm sells more inventory than it replaces. The result (in a typical inflationary environment) is lower COGS and higher profit. However, the increase in profit is not sustainable once the current inventory is depleted.

Results of Choice of Method

The choice of method affects numerous financial statement line items and their related financial ratios. Assuming price increases (i.e., inflation) and stable or increasing inventory quantities:

LIFO results in...	FIFO results in...
higher COGS	lower COGS
lower taxes	higher taxes
lower net income	higher net income
lower inventory balances	higher inventory balances
lower working capital	higher working capital
higher cash flows (less taxes)	lower cash flows (more taxes)
lower net and gross margins	higher net and gross margins
lower current ratio	higher current ratio
higher inventory turnover	lower inventory turnover
higher debt-to-equity	lower debt-to-equity

Inventory Valuation

Under IFRS, inventories are valued at the lower of cost or net realizable value. Inventory "write-ups" are allowed, but only to the extent that a previous write-down to net realizable value was recorded.

Under U.S. GAAP, inventories are valued at the lower of cost or market. Market is usually equal to replacement cost but cannot exceed net realizable value or be less than net realizable value minus a normal profit margin. No subsequent "write-up" is allowed.

Inventory Analysis

An increase in raw materials and/or work-in-process inventory may be an indication of an expected increase in demand. Conversely, an increase in finished goods inventory, while raw materials and work-in-process are decreasing, may be an indication of decreasing demand. Finished goods inventory that is growing faster than sales may be an indication of declining demand and, ultimately, excessive and potentially obsolete inventory.

THE CAPITALIZING VS. EXPENSING DECISION
Cross-Reference to CFA Institute Assigned Topic Review #17

When a firm makes an expenditure, it can either capitalize the cost as an asset on the balance sheet or expense the cost in the income statement. Capitalizing results in higher assets, higher equity, and higher operating cash flow compared to expensing. Capitalizing also results in higher earnings in the first year and lower earnings in subsequent years as the capitalized cost is depreciated.

Depreciation Methods

In the early years of an asset's life, accelerated depreciation will result in higher depreciation expense, lower net income, and lower ROA and ROE compared to straight-line depreciation. Cash flow is the same assuming tax depreciation is unaffected by the choice of method for financial reporting purposes. Firms can lower depreciation expense and increase net income by using longer useful lives and higher salvage values.

Impairment

Under IFRS, an asset is impaired when its carrying value exceeds the recoverable amount. The recoverable amount is the greater of fair value less selling costs and the value in use (present value of expected cash flows). If impaired, the asset is written-down to the recoverable amount. Loss recoveries are permitted. Under U.S. GAAP, an asset is impaired if its carrying value is greater than the asset's undiscounted future cash flows. If impaired, the asset is written-down to fair value. Subsequent recoveries are not allowed for assets held for use.

Asset impairments involve considerable management discretion. When the impairment loss is recognized, ROA and ROE will decrease. In subsequent periods, ROA and ROE will increase as a result of lower assets and lower equity. Impairments have no impact on cash flow. Under IFRS, firms have the option to revalue assets based on fair value. Revaluation under U.S. GAAP is not permitted.

Average Age of Fixed Assets

The average age of fixed assets can be compared to the average useful life to estimate the timing of a company's future capital expenditures.

- Average age (in years) = accumulated depreciation / annual depreciation expense.
- Average depreciable life = ending gross investment / annual depreciation expense.
- Remaining useful life = ending net investment / annual depreciation expense.

Finance and Operating Leases

A finance lease is, in substance, a purchase of an asset that is financed with debt. Finance lease expense consists of depreciation of the asset and interest on the loan. The finance lease payment consists of an operating outflow of cash (interest expense) and a financing outflow of cash (principal reduction). An operating lease is simply a rental arrangement. No asset or liability is reported by the lessee. The rental payment is reported as an expense and as an operating outflow of cash.

Compared to an operating lease, a finance lease will result in higher assets, liabilities, leverage ratios, operating cash flow, and operating income. A finance lease will result in lower net income in the early years of the lease, lower financing cash flows, and lower working capital and current ratio.

INTERCORPORATE INVESTMENTS
Cross-Reference to CFA Institute Assigned Topic Review #18

Accounting for Intercorporate Investments

Percentage of ownership is typically used as a practical guide to determine influence or control for financial reporting purposes. Figure 1 contains the guidelines used to determine which reporting method is required for intercorporate investments. The conceptual distinction for determining reporting methods centers on the degree to which the investee (affiliate) is an integral part of the investor (parent).

Figure 1: Accounting Standards for Intercorporate Investments

Ownership	Degree of Influence/Control	U.S. GAAP Method	IFRS Method
Less than 20%	No significant influence	Depends on security classification	Same as U.S. GAAP
20% to 50%	Significant influence	Equity method	Same as U.S. GAAP
Each party owns 50%	Shared control / joint venture	Equity method*	Same as U.S. GAAP
More than 50%	Control	Acquisition	Same as U.S. GAAP

* In rare cases, proportionate consolidation is allowed under U.S. GAAP and under IFRS.

Classifications of Financial Securities

- *Debt securities held-to-maturity* are securities of which a company has the positive *intent and ability* to hold to maturity. This classification applies only to debt securities; it does not apply to equity investments.
- *Debt and equity securities available-for-sale* may be sold to address the liquidity and other needs of a company.
- *Debt and equity trading securities* are securities acquired for the purpose of selling them in the near term.

Important financial statement effects of the classifications are summarized in Figure 2.

Figure 2: Accounting Treatment for Financial Securities Under U.S. GAAP and IFRS*

Classification	Management Intent	U.S. GAAP Balance Sheet Treatment	U.S. GAAP Income Statement Treatment	Difference Between U.S. GAAP and IFRS*
Trading securities	Acquired for the purpose of selling in the near-term.	Reported at fair market value.	Interest, dividends, realized and unrealized gains and losses reported.	No difference between U.S. GAAP and IFRS.
Available-for-sale securities	May be sold to address liquidity needs.	Reported at fair market value with unrealized gains and losses in comprehensive income in shareholders' equity.	Interest, dividends, and realized gains and losses reported.	Similar to U.S. GAAP, except unrealized foreign exchange gains/ losses on debt securities are recognized in the income statement under IFRS.
Held-to-maturity debt securities	Management has positive intent and ability to hold to maturity.	Reported at historical cost.	Interest and any realized gains and losses reported.	No difference between U.S. GAAP and IFRS.

* current IFRS

IFRS 9 (New standards)

IFRS 9 changes the terminology for the classification of investments in financial assets.

Amortized Cost (for Debt Securities Only)

Debt securities are accounted for using the amortized cost method if they meet both of the following criteria: (1) a business model test (the securities are being held to collect contractual cash flows) and (2) a cash flow characteristic test (contractual cash flows must be either principal or interest on principal).

Fair Value Through Profit or Loss (for Debt and Equity Securities)

Debt securities may be classified as *fair value through profit or loss* if either (1) they are held for trading or (2) accounting for those securities at amortized cost would result in an *accounting mismatch*. Equity securities that are held for trading must be classified as fair value through profit or loss. Other equity securities may be classified as either fair value through profit or loss, or fair value through OCI. Once classified, the choice is irrevocable.

Fair Value Through Other Comprehensive Income (for Equity Securities Only)

The accounting treatment under fair value through OCI is the same as under the previously used available-for-sale classification.

Reclassification under IFRS 9

Reclassification of equity securities under the new standards is not permitted as the initial designation (FVPL or FVOCI) is irrevocable. Reclassification of debt securities from amortized cost to FVPL (or vice versa) is permitted only if the business model has changed. Unrecognized gains/losses on debt securities carried at amortized cost and reclassified as FVPL are recognized in the income statement. Debt securities that are reclassified out of FVPL as measured at amortized cost are transferred at fair value on the transfer date, and that fair value becomes the carrying amount.

Equity Method

Under the *equity method*, the investment is listed at cost on the balance sheet. Dividends that are paid by the investee increase cash and decrease the investment account on the asset side of the balance sheet. In addition, the investor's pro rata share of the investee's net income increases the asset account and is listed as income on the investor's income statement.

Acquisition Method

Under the acquisition method, the balance sheets of the two entities are *consolidated* as follows: add together all asset and liability accounts net of intercorporate transfers; do not adjust the equity accounts of the parent; and list the minority interest as a separate component of stockholders' equity. Minority interest is equal to the proportion of the subsidiary that the parent does not own times the net equity of the subsidiary.

On the consolidated income statement, add the revenues and expenses of the parent and the subsidiary together as of the consolidation date. Subtract the minority shareholders' share of the subsidiary's net income from this amount. The minority interest amount on the income statement equals the proportion of the subsidiary the parent does not own multiplied by the net income of the subsidiary.

Effect of Choice of Method on Reported Financial Performance

There are four important effects on certain balance sheet and income statement items that result from the choice of accounting method (in most situations):

1. Both (equity and acquisition) methods report the same net income.

2. Compared to the equity method, acquisition method equity will be higher by the amount of minority interest.

3. Assets and liabilities are higher under the acquisition method compared to the equity method.

4. Sales and expenses are higher under the acquisition method compared to the equity method.

Assuming net income is positive, these effects generally result in the equity method reporting more favorable results compared to the acquisition method, as shown in Figure 3.

Figure 3: Differences in Reported Financial Results from Choice of Method

	Equity Method	*Acquisition*
Net profit margin*	Higher because sales are lower and net income is the same.	Lower
ROE*	Higher	Lower
ROA*	Higher because net income is the same and assets are lower.	Lower

*Assuming net income is positive.

Special Purpose Entities and Variable Interest Entities

A special purpose entity (SPE), also known as a special purchase vehicle or off-balance sheet entity, is a legal structure created to isolate certain assets and obligations of the sponsor. SPEs are usually formed to serve a specific purpose, so they are limited in scope. The typical motivation is to obtain low-cost financing. An SPE can take the form of a corporation, partnership, joint venture, or trust, although the entity does not necessarily have separate management or even employees.

The Financial Accounting Standards Board (FASB) coined the name variable interest entity (VIE) to identify an SPE that meets certain conditions set forth in FASB interpretation No. 46(R), "Consolidation of Variable Interest Entities" (FIN 46R). If an entity is considered a VIE under FIN 46(R), it must be consolidated by the primary beneficiary. According to FIN 46(R), a variable interest is a contractual, ownership, or other pecuniary interest in an entity that changes as a result of the fair value of the entity's net assets. The variable interest will absorb portions of the SPE's potential losses and receive portions of the potential residual returns.

Following are some examples of common variable interests and the potential risks and residual rewards:

- *At-risk equity investment.* The investor receives the residual benefits but also absorbs the potential losses.
- *Debt guarantee.* In the event of default, the guarantor will experience a loss.
- *Subordinated debt.* Since senior debt is repaid before subordinated debt, the subordinated debtholders absorb the loss in the event the senior debtholders cannot be repaid.
- *Lease residual guarantee.* The lessee guarantees the fair value of the asset at the end of the lease. If the fair value is less than the guaranteed amount, the lessee experiences a loss.
- *Participation rights.* The holder receives a predetermined share of the profit.
- *Asset purchase option.* The holder benefits from an increase in the fair value of the asset.

Consolidation Requirements

Figure 4 summarizes the conditions that identify a VIE.

Figure 4: Is an Entity a VIE?

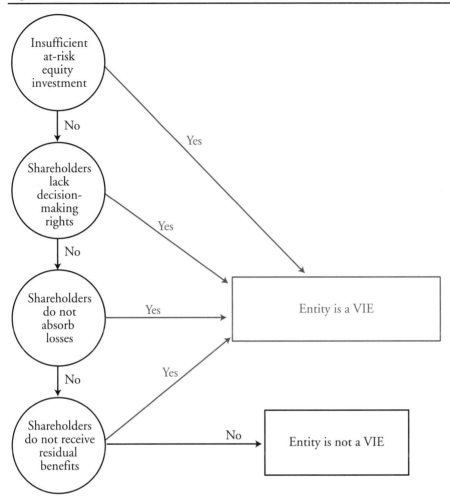

Once it is determined that an entity is a VIE, the entity must be consolidated. The firm that must consolidate the VIE is known as the primary beneficiary. The **primary beneficiary** is the entity that is exposed to the majority of the loss risks or receives the majority of the residual benefits, or both. Voting control is inconsequential at this point.

EMPLOYEE COMPENSATION: POST-EMPLOYMENT AND SHARE-BASED
Cross-Reference to CFA Institute Assigned Topic Review #19

The Pension Obligation for a Defined-Benefit Plan

The **projected benefit obligation** (PBO) is the actuarial present value (at the assumed discount rate) of all future pension benefits earned to date, based on expected future salary increases. It measures the value of the obligation assuming the firm is a going concern.

Reconciliation of Beginning and Ending PBO

Figure 5: Funded Status of a Pension Plan

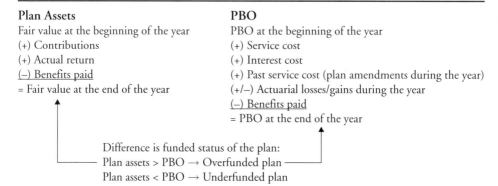

Plan Assets	PBO
Fair value at the beginning of the year	PBO at the beginning of the year
(+) Contributions	(+) Service cost
(+) Actual return	(+) Interest cost
(−) Benefits paid	(+) Past service cost (plan amendments during the year)
= Fair value at the end of the year	(+/−) Actuarial losses/gains during the year
	(−) Benefits paid
	= PBO at the end of the year

Difference is funded status of the plan:
Plan assets > PBO → Overfunded plan
Plan assets < PBO → Underfunded plan

Balance Sheet Effects

The funded status reflects the economic standing of a pension plan:

funded status = fair value of plan assets − PBO

The balance sheet presentation under both U.S. GAAP and IFRS is as follows:

balance sheet asset (liability) = funded status

Pension Expense Components

Figure 6: Difference Between Recognition of Components of Pension Costs Under U.S. GAAP and IFRS

Component	U.S. GAAP	IFRS
Current service cost	Income statement	Income statement
Past service cost	OCI, amortized over service life	Income statement
Interest cost	Income statement	Income statement
Expected return	Income statement	Income statement*
Actuarial gains/losses	Amortized portion in income statement. Unamortized in OCI.	All in OCI—not amortized (called 'Remeasurements')

* Under IFRS, the expected rate of return on plan assets equals the discount rate and net interest expense/income is reported.

Additional explanation for these components follows:

- *Service cost:* increase in the PBO reflecting the pension benefits earned during the year.
- *Interest cost:* increase in PBO resulting from interest owed on the current benefit obligation.
- *Expected return on plan assets:* Under U.S. GAAP, assumed long run rate of return on plan assets used to smooth the volatility that would be caused by using actual returns. Under IFRS, expected rate of return on plan assets is implicitly equal to the discount rate used for computing PBO.
- *Amortization of unrecognized prior service cost:* amortized costs for changes in the PBO that result from amendments to the plan (under U.S. GAAP only). Under IFRS, prior service costs are expensed immediately and not amortized.
- *Amortization and deferral of gains or losses:* amortization of gains and losses caused by (1) changes in actuarial assumptions and (2) differences between actual and expected return on plan assets. Under U.S. GAAP, actuarial gains and losses are recognized in OCI and amortized using the corridor method. Under IFRS, actuarial gains and losses (called remeasurements) are recognized in OCI and not amortized.

Total Periodic Pension Cost

Analysts often calculate **total periodic pension cost** (TPPC) by eliminating the smoothing amounts and including the *actual* return on assets. The result is a more volatile measure of pension expense. TPPC includes pension expense recognized in the income statement and pension cost that bypasses income statement (i.e., recognized in OCI). While TPPC calculated under U.S. GAAP is the same as that calculated under IFRS, the allocation between income statement and OCI differs.

TPPC can be calculated by computing increase in PBO for the period (adjusted for benefits payments) and then subtracting the actual return on assets.

> TPPC = ending PBO – beginning PBO + benefits paid – actual return on plan assets

Alternatively, TPPC is equal to the contributions minus the change in funded status during the year.

> TPPC = contributions – (ending funded status – beginning funded status)

Fundamental Pension Assumptions

The company must make and disclose three actuarial assumptions in the pension footnotes:

1. The **discount rate** is the interest rate used to compute the present value of the pension obligations. This is the interest rate at which the company could settle its pension obligation. Notice that this is not the risk-free rate.

2. The **rate of compensation increase** is the average annual rate at which employee compensation is expected to increase over time.

3. The **expected return on plan assets** (U.S. GAAP only) is the long-term assumed rate of return on the investments in the plan. Using an expected long-run return assumption rather than actual returns serves to smooth the net pension expense calculation.

Any changes in assumptions that might cause only a small change in the total pension obligation itself can still have a large impact on the net pension asset or liability. The same is true with pension expense; because it is a net amount (service and interest cost net of expected return on plan assets), relatively minor changes in the assumptions can have a major impact on reported pension expense.

Assumptions of high discount rates, low compensation growth rates, and high expected rates of return on plan assets will decrease pension expense, increase earnings, and reduce the pension liability. The more aggressive these assumptions are, the lower the earnings quality of the firm.

The use of a lower rate of compensation growth will improve reported results because it will result in the following:

- Lower estimated future pension payments and, hence, a lower PBO.
- Lower service cost and a lower interest cost; thus, pension expense will decrease.

Figure 7: Effect of Changes in Assumptions

Effect on...	Increase Discount Rate	Decrease Rate of Compensation Growth	Increase Expected Rate of Return
Balance Sheet Liability	Decrease	Decrease	No effect
Total Periodic Pension Cost	Decrease*	Decrease	No effect
Periodic pension cost in P&L	Decrease*	Decrease	Decrease**

* For mature plans, a higher discount rate might increase interest costs. In rare cases, interest cost will increase by enough to offset the decrease in the current service cost, and periodic pension cost will increase.

** Under U.S. GAAP only. Not applicable under IFRS.

Non-Pension Postretirement Benefits

Accounting for *non-pension* postretirement benefits is very similar to accounting for pension benefits, with the following differences:

- The accumulated postretirement benefit obligation (APBO) is the actuarial present value of the expected postretirement benefits. It is estimated using a discount rate applied specifically to those benefits.
- Many postretirement benefit plans are unfunded, which means there are no plan assets, employer contributions equal benefits paid, and the funded status equals the APBO.

SHARE-BASED COMPENSATION

This topic review provides a brief discussion of the key features of the latest standard on accounting for stock-based compensation plans. The key result is that firms must now report compensation expense related to stock option plans on the income statement based on the option's value at issuance. This can significantly decrease reported earnings.

According to SFAS No. 123(R), firms are required to recognize compensation expense based on the fair value of share-based awards as of the grant date. The fair value is estimated using an option pricing model. This expense is amortized over the period required for vesting of the options (i.e., the service period).

MULTINATIONAL OPERATIONS
Cross-Reference to CFA Institute Assigned Topic Review #20

Transaction Exposure

Transactions denominated in foreign currencies are measured in the presentation (reporting) currency at the spot rate on the transaction date. If the exchange rate changes, a gain or loss is recognized on the settlement date. If the balance sheet date occurs before the transaction is settled, the gain or loss is based on the exchange rate on the balance sheet date. After the transaction has settled, additional gain or loss is recognized if the exchange rate changes after the balance sheet date.

Translation of foreign currency denominated financial statements of subsidiaries

From a financial statement analysis view, there are two tasks that must be understood in multinational operations. First, you must know and be able to apply two different methods of consolidating foreign subsidiaries' operating results into the parent's financial statements. Second, you must understand how these two different accounting procedures affect the parent's financial statements and ratios.

The two methods of consolidation are the *temporal method* (sometimes also referred to as *remeasurement*) and the *current rate method* (a.k.a. *translation*). The appropriate method depends on the subsidiary's functional currency (i.e., the currency in which the subsidiary generates and expends most of its cash). The rules that govern the determination of the functional currency under SFAS 52 are as follows:

- The results of operations, financial position, and cash flows of all foreign operations must be measured in the designated functional currency.
- Self-contained, independent subsidiaries whose operations are primarily located in the local market will use the local currency as the functional currency.
- Subsidiaries whose operations are well integrated with the parent will use the parent's currency as the functional currency.
- If the functional currency is the local currency, use the current rate method.
- If the functional currency is the parent's currency or some other currency, use the temporal method.

Figure 8: Three Methods for Remeasurement/Translation of Local Currencies

Translation: Current Rate Method — Remeasurement: Temporal Method — Current Rate/ Temporal Method

When consolidating the results of foreign subsidiaries, it is important to decide which exchange rate should be used for each account. There are essentially three choices: (1) the current exchange rate, (2) the average exchange rate over the reporting period, and (3) the historical exchange rate (which is the rate that existed when a particular transaction occurred). Which you use depends on which method is appropriate. Study and memorize the information contained in Figure 9.

Figure 9: Exchange Rate Usage Under the Temporal and Current Rate Methods

Account	Rate Used to Translate Account Using the…	
	Temporal Method	*Current Rate Method*
Monetary assets/liabilities	Current rate	Current rate
Nonmonetary assets/liabilities	Historical rate	Current rate
Common stock	Historical rate	Historical rate
Equity (taken as a whole)	Mixed*	Current rate**
Revenues and SG&A	Average rate	Average rate
Cost of good sold	Historical rate	Average rate
Depreciation	Historical rate	Average rate
Net income	Mixed*	Average rate
Exposure	Net monetary assets	Shareholders' equity
Exchange rate gain or loss	Income statement	Equity

*   Net income is a "mixed rate" under the temporal method because (1) the FX translation gain or loss is shown on the income statement, (2) revenues and SG&A are remeasured at average, while (3) COGS and depreciation are remeasured at historical. Equity is "mixed" because the change in retained earnings (which includes net income) is posted to the equity accounts.

**   Under the current rate method, total assets and liabilities are translated at the current rate. The total equity (equity taken as a whole) would then have to be translated at the current rate for the balance sheet to balance.

Calculating the Translation Gain or Loss

Translation gains or losses result from gains or losses related to balance sheet accounts that are translated at the current rate (i.e., they are exposed to changes in exchange rates).

Under the current rate method, all assets and liabilities are translated at the current rate, so the net exposure is assets minus liabilities, or total shareholders' equity:

> exposure under the current rate method = shareholders' equity

Under the temporal method, only cash, accounts receivable, accounts payable, current debt, and long-term debt are translated at the current rate (remember that inventory and fixed assets are translated at the historical rate):

> exposure under the temporal method = (cash + accounts receivable)
> – (accounts payable + current debt + long-term debt) = net monetary assets

Under the current rate method, the translation gains/losses are accumulated on the balance sheet in the equity section as part of comprehensive income in an account called the **cumulative translation adjustment** (CTA).

Under the temporal method, no CTA is reported in shareholders' equity. Instead, the remeasurement gain or loss is recognized in the income statement.

Comparing Subsidiary Results to Translated Results (Current Rate Method)

On the exam, remember these key points regarding the original versus the translated financial statements and ratios.

- Pure balance sheet and pure income statement ratios will be the same.
- If the LC is depreciating, translated mixed ratios (with an income statement item in the numerator and an end-of-period balance sheet item in the denominator) will be larger than the original ratio.
- If the LC is appreciating, translated mixed ratios (with an income statement item in the numerator and an end-of-period balance sheet item in the denominator) will be smaller than the original ratio.

Comparing Results Using the Temporal and Current Rate Methods

The effects on a selected set of ratios of the choice between the current rate and temporal methods are shown in Figure 8.

Figure 10: Effect of Translation Methods on Selected Financial Ratios

	Appreciating Local Currency		Depreciating Local Currency	
	Temporal	Current Rate	Temporal	Current Rate
*Liquidity Ratios**				
Current ratio (assuming subsidiary has inventory)	Lower	Higher	Higher	Lower
Quick ratio	Same	Same	Same	Same
A/R turnover	Same	Same	Same	Same
Inventory turnover	Uncertain	Uncertain	Uncertain	Uncertain
*Operating Efficiency Ratios**				
Fixed asset turnover	Higher	Lower	Lower	Higher
Total asset turnover	Higher	Lower	Lower	Higher
*Profitability Ratios**				
Gross profit margin	Higher	Lower	Lower	Higher
Net profit margin	Uncertain	Uncertain	Uncertain	Uncertain
ROE	Uncertain	Uncertain	Uncertain	Uncertain
ROA	Uncertain	Uncertain	Uncertain	Uncertain
*Financial Leverage Ratios**				
Interest coverage	Higher	Lower	Lower	Higher
LTD-to-total capital	Higher	Lower	Lower	Higher

* Ratios are calculated using end-of-period balance sheet numbers.

Effective Tax Rate

Earnings of multinational companies are subject to multiple tax jurisdictions, so the **effective tax rate** often differs from the **statutory tax rate**. Expected changes in the mix of profits from different countries can be used by the analyst to forecast future tax expenses for the company.

Earnings Sustainability

Revenues of multinational companies may be denominated in different currencies but are translated into the reporting currency for the purpose of preparing financial statements. Revenue growth can occur due to price and volume changes, or due to changes in exchange rates. Analysts separate the two because the growth in revenues due to changes in price and/or volume is considered more sustainable.

EVALUATING QUALITY OF FINANCIAL REPORTS

Cross-Reference to CFA Institute Assigned Topic Review #21

It is important for an analyst to evaluate the quality of a company's financial reports before relying on them for investment decision making.

High-quality reporting provides decision-useful information, which is information that is accurate as well as relevant. High-quality earnings are sustainable and meet the required return on investment. High-quality earnings assume high-quality reporting.

The conceptual framework for assessing the quality of a company's reports entails answering two questions:

1. Are the underlying financial reports GAAP compliant and decision-useful?

2. Are the earnings of high quality?

Potential Problems that Affect the Quality of Financial Reports

Potential problems that affect the quality of financial reports can result from:

1. Measurement and timing issues, and/or

2. Classification issues.

Additionally, biased accounting and accounting for business combinations can compromise the quality of financial reports. *GAAP compliance is a necessary, but not sufficient, condition for high-quality financial reporting.*

Quantitative Models

The Beneish model is used to estimate the probability of earnings manipulation and is based on eight key variables. However, as managers become aware of the use of such models, they are likely to game the model's inputs. This concern is

©2016 Kaplan, Inc.

supported by an observed decline in the predictive power of the Beneish model over time.

High-Quality Earnings

Sustainable or persistent earnings are those that are expected to recur in the future. Earnings with a high proportion of nonrecurring items are considered to be nonsustainable (and, hence, low quality).

High-quality earnings are characterized by two elements:

1. Sustainable: high-quality earnings are expected to recur in future periods.

2. Adequate: high-quality earnings cover the company's cost of capital.

There are two major contributors to earnings manipulation:

1. Revenue recognition issues.

2. Expense recognition issues (capitalization).

Bill-and-hold sales, or channel stuffing, are examples of aggressive revenue recognition practices. Analysis of days' sales outstanding (DSO) and receivables turnover (over time and compared to peers) is used to reveal red flags. Cost capitalization will result in an excessive asset base, which can be spotted by evaluation of the trend and comparative analysis of common-size balance sheets.

Mean Reversion in Earnings

Mean reversion in earnings, or the tendency of earnings at extreme levels to revert back to normal levels over time, implies that earnings at very high levels are not sustainable. Mean reversion is quicker for accruals-based earnings and faster still if such accruals are discretionary.

Evaluating the Earnings Quality of a Company

Indicators of cash flow quality

High-quality cash flow means that the reported cash flow was high (i.e., good economic performance), and the underlying reporting quality was also high.

Elements to check for in the statement of cash flows:

- Unusual items or items that have not shown up in prior years.
- Excessive outflows for receivables and inventory due to aggressive revenue recognition.
- Provisions for, and reversals of, restructuring charges.

Indicators of balance sheet quality

High financial reporting quality for a balance sheet is evidenced by completeness, unbiased measurement, and clarity of presentation.

Completeness of a balance sheet can be compromised by the existence of off-balance sheet liabilities. Also, biased measurement may be present in the measurement of pension obligations, goodwill, investments, inventory, and other assets.

INTEGRATION OF FSA TECHNIQUES
Cross-Reference to CFA Institute Assigned Topic Review #22

Financial Analysis Framework

The basic financial analysis framework involves:

1. Establishing objectives.

2. Collecting data.

3. Processing data.

4. Analyzing data.

5. Developing and communicating conclusions.

6. Following up.

Integration of FSA Techniques

1. Use the extended DuPont equation to examine the sources of earnings and performance.

2. Remove equity income from associates and the investment account to eliminate any bias.

3. Examine the composition of the balance sheet over time.

4. Determine if the capital structure can support future obligations and strategic plans by analyzing the components of long-term capital. Note that some liabilities don't necessarily result in an outflow of cash.

5. Segment disclosures are valuable in identifying the contribution to revenue and profit of each segment. Note the relationship between capital expenditures by segment and segment rates of return in order to evaluate capital spending decisions.

6. The balance sheet should be adjusted for off-balance-sheet financing activities. Capitalize operating leases for analytical purposes by increasing assets and liabilities by the present value of the remaining lease payments. Also, adjust the income statement by replacing rent expense with depreciation expense on the lease asset and interest expense on the lease liability.

7. Users must be aware of the proposed changes in accounting standards because of the financial statement effects and the potential impact on a firm's valuation. Earnings can be disaggregated into cash flow and accruals using either a balance sheet approach or a cash flow statement approach. For either measure, the lower the accruals ratio, the higher the earnings quality.

8. Earnings are considered higher quality when confirmed by cash flow. Cash flow can be compared to operating profit by adding back cash paid for interest and taxes to operating cash flow.

9. The standalone market value of a firm can be computed by eliminating the pro-rata market value of investments in associates. An implied P/E multiple can be computed by dividing the standalone market value by earnings not including equity income from associates.

Figure 11: Major Differences (in CFA Level II Curriculum) Between IFRS and U.S. GAAP Treatment

Topic Area	IFRS	U.S. GAAP
Accounting for Inventories		
Cost flow assumption	LIFO not allowed	LIFO allowed
Valuation	Valued at lower of cost or net realizable value (NRV)	Valued at lower of cost or market. Market is subject to an upper bound of NRV and lower bound of (NRV – profit margin).
Writedown	If NRV falls below cost, a reversible impairment loss is recognized in income statement.	If market value is lower than cost, an irreversible impairment loss is recognized in income statement.
Long Lived Assets		
Research and development	Research costs are expensed, while development costs are capitalized.	Both research and development costs are expensed with some exceptions.
Impairments	1-step process	2-step process
Revaluation	Allowed for assets carried at fair value	Generally prohibited
Intercorporate Investments		
Passive investments	Unrealized gains and losses on available-for-sale debt securities attributable to forex movements is recognized in income statement.	All unrealized gains and losses on available-for-sale securities are recognized in OCI.
Reclassification of passive investments	Restricts reclassification into and out of fair value through profit or loss	No such restriction
Impairment losses on passive investments	Reversal of impairments on debt securities allowed if attributed to specific event	No reversal of impairment losses
Investment in associates	Fair value accounting only allowed for venture capital, mutual funds, and similar entities	Fair value accounting allowed for all
Acquisition method— goodwill computation	Partial or full goodwill allowed	Only full goodwill allowed
Goodwill impairment	1-step process	2-step process
Acquisition method— recognition of contingent assets	Not allowed	Allowed

Figure 11: Major Differences (in CFA Level II Curriculum) Between IFRS and U.S. GAAP Treatment

Topic Area	IFRS	U.S. GAAP
Pension Accounting		
Balance sheet and total periodic pension cost	Both IFRS and U.S. GAAP report funded status on the balance sheet. Total periodic pension cost is same for both IFRS and GAAP, but the allocation to income statement and OCI differs.	
Pension cost in P&L vs. OCI	1. Prior service cost expensed 2. Discount rate = expected rate of return 3. Remeasurements in OCI and not amortized	1. Prior service cost in OCI and amortized 2. Expected rate of return does not have to be same as discount rate 3. Actuarial gains/losses in OCI and amortized using corridor approach
Multinational Operations		
Subsidiaries in hyperinflationary economies	Restate LC financial statements for inflation (nonmonetary assets/liabilities indexed to inflation). Convert restated financial statements at current rate. Purchasing power gains/losses in income statement.	Use temporal method
Cash flow statement		
Dividend/interest income and interest expense	Can be classified as operating or financing cash flows.	Must be classified as operating cash flows.

CORPORATE FINANCE

| Topic Weight on Exam | 5–15% |
| SchweserNotes™ Reference | Book 2, Pages 221–397 |

CAPITAL BUDGETING
Cross-Reference to CFA Institute Assigned Topic Review #23

Know the definitions of cash flow and the basic computations for expansion and replacement projects. For either type of project, we need to calculate the initial outlay (at t = 0), the annual incremental after-tax operating cash flows (t = 1,...,n), and any additional terminal year cash flows (t = n).

Cash Flow Estimation for Expansion Projects

For an *expansion project*, the components of these cash flows are as follows:

Initial investment outlay. May include purchase price plus transportation and installation costs, additional costs such as training, and any required increase in net working capital.

After-tax operating cash flow (CF). Calculated as either of the following:

$$CF = (S - C - D)(1 - T) + D$$

$$= (S - C)(1 - T) + (TD)$$

where:
S = sales
C = cash operating costs
D = depreciation expense
T = marginal tax rate

Terminal year after-tax non-operating cash flow (TNOCF). Add the after-tax salvage value of the assets and any recapture of net working capital to the final year's after-tax operating cash flow.

$$TNOCF = Sal_T + NWCInv - T\,(Sal_T - B_T)$$

where:
Sal_T = cash proceeds from sale of fixed capital
B_T = book value of fixed capital

Cash Flow Estimation for Replacement Projects

For a *replacement project*, the process is similar, but:

- You must reduce the initial outlay by the after-tax proceeds of the sale of the existing asset.
- You must use only the *change* in depreciation that results from replacement.

If the new equipment has an expected life equal to the remaining life of the equipment to be replaced, then a positive NPV or IRR greater than the project cost of capital is sufficient to decide to replace the existing assets.

Be aware that the tax implications of the sale of assets can increase or decrease cash flow. If the sale price is greater than the carrying cost (book value) of the asset, tax must be paid on the gain; this decreases the after-tax sale proceeds. If the sale price is less than the book value, then taxes are reduced (and cash flow increased) by the tax rate times the amount of the loss.

Some points to remember in estimating incremental after-tax cash flows:

- Ignore sunk costs (any costs that are unaffected by the accept/reject decision).
- Ignore any financing costs associated with asset purchase (financing costs are included in the project cost of capital or WACC).
- Include any effects on the cash flows for other firm products (externalities).
- Include the opportunity cost (actual cash flows lost) of using any existing firm assets for the project.
- Shipping and installation costs are included in the initial cost used to calculate the annual depreciation for new assets.

Mutually Exclusive Projects With Unequal Lives

For *mutually exclusive projects with unequal lives*, the fact that the longer-lived project has a higher NPV is not sufficient to justify its acceptance.

There are two approaches to put the projects on an equal basis timewise:

The replacement chain approach. Assume that the shorter project will be repeated until the total number of years is equal to the years for the longer project. If we are comparing a 3-year and a 6-year project, we would project the cash flows as if we repeated the 3-year project at the end of year 3 and sum the cash flows to create a 6-year project for comparison.

We can then directly compare the NPV of the repeated project to the project with an expected life of six years and accept the one with the greater NPV (as long as the NPV is positive).

The equivalent annual annuity (EAA) *approach.* An alternative to the replacement chain approach is to convert the NPV for each project into an equivalent annual payment and select the project with the greater (positive) equivalent annual payment.

For a 3-year project with a net present value of NPV(3), the steps are as follows:

PV = NPV(3); FV = 0; N = 3; I/Y = WACC or project cost of capital; and compute PMT, which is the EAA of the 3-year project.

For a 6-year project with a net present value of NPV(6), the steps are as follows:

PV = NPV(6); FV = 0; N = 6; I/Y = WACC or project cost of capital; and compute PMT, which is the EAA of the 6-year project.

Project Risk Analysis

There are three techniques for estimating the stand-alone risk of a capital investment/project:

- *Sensitivity analysis.* Involves changing a variable such as sales volume, sales price, input cost, or the assumed cost of capital, and recalculating the NPV. The project with the greater percentage change in NPV for a given variable change is the riskier project.
- *Scenario analysis.* Calculate the NPV for "base-case," worst-case (low sales, low price, etc.), and a best-case scenario and assign probabilities to each of these outcomes. Then calculate the standard deviation of the NPV as you would with any probability model.

- *Monte Carlo simulation.* Use assumed probability distributions for the key variables in the NPV calculation, draw random values for these variables and calculate NPV (thousands of times), and use the distribution of NPVs to estimate the expected NPV and the standard deviation of NPV as a measure of stand-alone project risk.

Capital Rationing

Ideally, firms will continue to invest in positive return NPV projects until the marginal returns equal the marginal cost of capital. If a firm has insufficient capital to do this, it must ration its capital (allocate its funds) among the best possible combination of acceptable projects.

Capital rationing is the allocation of a fixed amount of capital among the set of available projects that will maximize shareholder wealth. A firm with less capital than profitable (i.e., positive NPV) projects should choose the combination of projects it can afford to fund that has the greatest total NPV. Remember, the goal with capital rationing is to maximize the overall NPV within the capital budget, not necessarily to select the individual projects with the highest NPV.

Using CAPM to Determine the Discount Rate

The CAPM can be used to determine the appropriate discount rate for a project based on risk. The project beta, $\beta_{project}$, is used as a measure of the systematic risk of the project, and the security market line (SML) estimates the project's required return as:

$$R_{project} = R_f + \beta_{project} [E(R_M) - R_f]$$

Real Options

Real options are similar to financial call and put options in that they give the option holder the right, but not the obligation, to make a decision. The difference is that real options are based on real assets rather than financial assets and are contingent on future events. Real options offer managers flexibility that can increase the NPV of individual projects.

Types of real options include the following:

- Timing options.
- Abandonment options.
- Expansion options.

- Flexibility options (price-setting and production-flexibility options).
- Fundamental options.

Approaches to Evaluating the Profitability of Real Options

- *Determine the NPV of the project without the option.* If the NPV of the project without the option is positive, the analyst knows that the project with the option must be even more valuable, and determining a specific value for the option is unnecessary.
- *Calculate the project NPV without the option and add the estimated value of the real option.*
- *Use decision trees.*
- *Use option pricing models.* Option pricing models are discussed in Study Session 17.

Accounting Income and Economic Income

Economic income is equal to the after-tax cash flow plus the change in the investment's market value. Interest is ignored and is instead included as a component of the discount rate.

> economic income = after-tax cash flow – economic depreciation

> where:
> economic depreciation = (beginning market value – ending market value)

The economic income rate of return for each year (economic income/beginning market value) is equal to the project's required rate of return. This makes sense because the required return is the discount rate used to determine the value of the investment.

Accounting income is the reported net income on a company's financial statements that results from an investment in a project.

There are two key factors that account for the *differences between economic and accounting income:*

1. Accounting depreciation is based on the original cost of the investment, while economic depreciation is based on the change in market value of the investment.

2. The after-tax cost of debt (interest expense) is subtracted from net income, while financing costs for determining economic income are reflected in the discount rate.

Other Valuation Models

Alternative forms of determining income should theoretically lead to the same calculated NPV if applied correctly.

- *Economic profit* is calculated as NOPAT – $WACC. Economic profit reflects the income earned by all capital holders and is therefore discounted at the WACC to determine the market value added (MVA), or NPV, of the investment.
- *Residual income* is focused on returns to equity holders and is calculated as net income less an equity charge. Residual income reflects the income to equity holders only and is discounted at the required return on equity to determine NPV.
- *Claims valuation* separates cash flows based on the claims that equity holders and debt holders have on the asset. Cash flows to debt holders are discounted at the cost of debt, and cash flows to equity holders are discounted at the cost of equity. The present value of each set of cash flows is added together to determine the value of the firm.

Economic profit models and residual income models are discussed in more detail in Study Session 12.

CAPITAL STRUCTURE AND LEVERAGE
Cross-Reference to CFA Institute Assigned Topic Review #24

Objective of the Capital Structure Decision

The objective of a company's *capital structure decision* is to determine the optimal proportion of debt and equity financing that will minimize the firm's weighted average cost of capital (WACC). This is also the capital structure that will maximize the value of the firm.

Capital Structure Theory

MM Proposition I (No Taxes)—capital structure is irrelevant; value of the firm is unaffected by the capital structure. $V_L = V_U$

MM Proposition II (No Taxes)—the cost of equity increases linearly as a company increases its proportion of debt financing. The benefits from using more debt are exactly offset by the rise in the cost of equity, resulting in no change in the firm's WACC.

Figure 1: MM Proposition II (No Taxes)

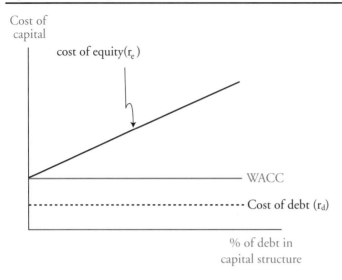

MM Proposition I (With Taxes)—Value is maximized at 100% debt; the tax shield provided by debt causes the WACC to decline as leverage increases.

$$V_L = V_U + (t \times d)$$

MM Proposition II (With Taxes)—WACC is minimized at 100% debt; the tax shield provided by debt causes the WACC to decline as leverage increases.

Figure 2: MM Proposition II (With Taxes)

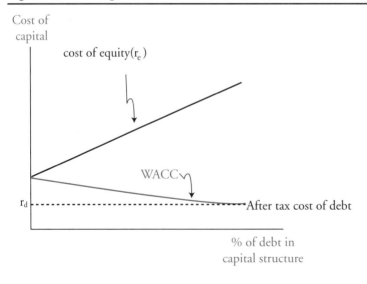

Costs and Their Potential Effect on the Capital Structure

Costs of financial distress are the increased costs companies face when earnings decline and the company has trouble paying its interest costs. The expected costs of financial distress for a firm have two components:

1. Direct and indirect costs of financial distress and bankruptcy.
2. Probability of financial distress.

In general, higher amounts of leverage result in greater expected costs of financial distress and a higher probability of financial distress.

The **net agency costs** of equity are the costs associated with the conflict of interest between a company's managers and owners, and consist of three components:

1. Monitoring costs.
2. Bonding costs.
3. Residual losses.

Costs of *asymmetric information* result from managers having more information about a firm than investors.

The Capital Structure Decision

With regard to management's decisions regarding capital structure:

- *MM's propositions with no taxes* says that capital structure is irrelevant.
- *MM's propositions with taxes* says that the tax shield provided by interest expense makes borrowing valuable, and the value of the firm is maximized, and the WACC is minimized, at 100% debt.
- *Pecking order theory* states that managers prefer financing choices that send the least visible signal to investors, with internal capital being most preferred, debt being next, and raising equity externally the least preferred method of financing.
- *Static trade-off theory* states that managers will try to balance the benefits of debt with the costs of financial distress. The static trade-off theory seeks to balance the costs of financial distress with the tax shield benefits from using debt, and states there is an optimal capital structure that has an optimal proportion of debt.

If we remove the assumption that there are no costs of financial distress, there comes a point where the additional value added by the tax shield from borrowing another dollar is exceeded by the value-reducing expected costs of financial distress from the additional borrowing. This point represents the optimal capital structure for a firm where the WACC is minimized as the value of the firm is maximized.

Accounting for the costs of financial distress, the expression for the value of a levered firm becomes:

$$V_L = V_U + (t \times d) - PV(\text{costs of financial distress})$$

Note that the previous equation and Figure 3 represent the static trade-off theory just discussed.

Figure 3: Static Trade-Off Theory: Firm Value vs. Capital Structure

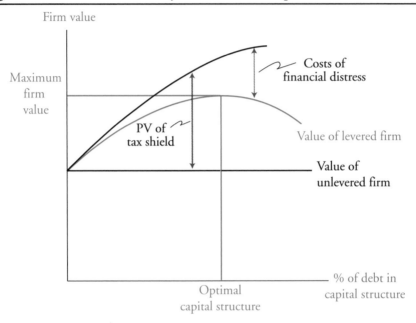

Factors to Consider for Analysis

Factors an analyst should consider when evaluating a firm's capital structure include:

- Changes in the firm's capital structure over time.
- Capital structure of competitors with similar business risk.
- Factors affecting agency costs such as the quality of corporate governance.

International Differences

Major factors that influence *international differences* in financial leverage include:

- Institutional, legal, and taxation factors.
- Financial market and banking system factors.
- Macroeconomic factors.

Figure 4: Impact of Country-Specific Factors on Capital Structure

Country Specific Factor	Use of Total Debt	Maturity of Debt
Institutional and Legal Factors		
Strong legal system	Lower	Longer
Less information asymmetry	Lower	Longer
Favorable tax rates on dividends	Lower	N/A
Financial Market Factors		
More liquid stock and bond markets	N/A	Longer
Greater reliance on banking system	Higher	N/A
Greater institutional investor presence	Lower	Longer
Macroeconomic Factors		
Higher inflation	Lower	Shorter
Higher GDP growth	N/A	Longer

DIVIDENDS AND DIVIDEND POLICY
Cross-Reference to CFA Institute Assigned Topic Review #25

Dividend Theories

Merton Miller and Franco Modigliani (MM) maintain that *dividend policy* is irrelevant, as it has no effect on the price of a firm's stock or its cost of capital. MM's argument of dividend irrelevance is based on their concept of *homemade dividends*. Dividend preference theory says investors prefer the certainty of current cash to future capital gains. Tax aversion theory states that investors are tax averse to dividends and would prefer companies instead buy back shares, especially when the tax rate on dividends is higher than the tax rate on capital gains.

Signaling Effect

The signaling effect of dividend changes is based on the idea that dividends convey information about future earnings from management to investors (who have less information about a firm's prospects than management). In general, unexpected increases are good news and unexpected decreases are bad news as seen by U.S. investors.

Clientele Effect

Clientele effect refers to the varying preferences for dividends of different groups of investors, such as individuals, institutions, and corporations. Companies structure their dividend policies consistent with preferences of their clienteles. Miller and Modigliani, however, note that once all the clienteles are satisfied, changing the dividend policy would only entail changing clienteles and would not affect firm value.

Taxation

A **double-taxation system** is used in the United States to tax dividends paid. Earnings are taxed at the corporate level regardless of whether they are distributed as dividends, and dividends are taxed again at the shareholder level.

$$\text{effective rate} = \text{corporate tax rate} + (1 - \text{corporate tax rate}) \times (\text{individual tax rate})$$

A **split-rate** corporate tax system taxes earnings distributed as dividends at a lower rate than earnings that are retained. The effect is to offset the higher (double) tax rate applied to dividends at the individual level.

Under an **imputation tax system**, taxes are paid at the corporate level but are attributed to the shareholder, so that *all taxes are effectively paid at the shareholder rate.*

Stable Dividend Policy

A firm with a stable dividend policy could use a target payout adjustment model to gradually move towards its target payout.

$$\text{expected dividend} = \begin{pmatrix} \text{previous} \\ \text{dividend} \end{pmatrix} + \left[\begin{pmatrix} \text{expected} \\ \text{increase} \\ \text{in EPS} \end{pmatrix} \times \begin{pmatrix} \text{target} \\ \text{payout} \\ \text{ratio} \end{pmatrix} \times \begin{pmatrix} \text{adjustment} \\ \text{factor} \end{pmatrix} \right]$$

where:
adjustment factor = 1 / number of years over which the adjustment in dividends will take place

Share Repurchases

There are five common rationales for share repurchases (versus dividends):

1. Potential tax advantages: When capital gains are taxed favorably compared to dividends.

2. Share price support/signaling: Management wants to signal better prospects for the firm.

3. Added flexibility: Reduces the need for "sticky" dividends in the future.

4. Offsets dilution from employee stock options.

5. Increases financial leverage by reducing equity in the balance sheet.

Dividend Coverage Ratios

The two most important predictors of dividend reliability are:

dividend coverage ratio = net income / dividends

FCFE coverage ratio = FCFE / (dividends + share repurchases)

CORPORATE PERFORMANCE, GOVERNANCE, AND BUSINESS ETHICS
Cross-Reference to CFA Institute Assigned Topic Review #26

Stakeholder Impact Analysis (SIA)

The SIA should:
- Identify the relevant stakeholders.
- Identify the critical interests and desires of each group.
- Identify the demands of each group on the company.
- Prioritize the importance of various stakeholders to the company.
- Provide a business strategy to meet the critical demands.

Principal-Agent Relationship Problems

The principal-agent relationship (PAR) arises when one group delegates decision making or control to another group. A PAR can create problems because the group receiving the power (i.e., the agent) generally has an asymmetric information advantage over the group delegating the power (i.e., the principal). The PAR problem emerges when the agent uses the information advantage to further their own interests to the detriment of the interests of the principal.

Principals should develop corporate governance procedures that:

- Affect the behavior of agents by setting goals and principles of behavior.
- Reduce information asymmetry.
- Remove agents who misbehave and/or behave unethically.

The Roots of Unethical Behavior

Unethical behavior arises from a variety of causes:

- Agents whose personal ethics are flawed are more likely to violate business ethics. Strong personal ethics are likely to lead to good business ethics.
- A simple failure to realize that an issue may lead to an ethics violation. Asking whether each decision has ethical implications will encourage business ethics.
- A culture focused only on profit and growth. Asking if it is ethical and profitable will encourage business ethics.
- A flawed business culture where top management sets unrealistic goals leads to unethical behavior. Ethical leadership formulates and communicates expectations that include sound ethical behavior.

Theories of Ethical Decision Making

The *Friedman Doctrine* narrowly addresses the social responsibility of business and concludes that the only social responsibility is to increase profits "within the rules of the game," meaning through "open and fair competition without deception or fraud."

Utilitarianism argues that business must weigh the consequences of each of their actions to society and seek to produce the highest good for the largest number of people.

Kantian ethics argues that people are different from other factors of production; they are more than just an economic input and deserve dignity and respect.

Rights theory argues that all individuals have fundamental rights and privileges. The greatest good of utilitarianism cannot come in violation of these fundamental rights of others.

Justice theories focus on a just distribution of economic output. John Rawls argued that justice is met if all participants would agree the rules are fair if the results would be acceptable when decided under a "veil of ignorance."

CORPORATE GOVERNANCE
Cross-Reference to CFA Institute Assigned Topic Review #27

Corporate governance is defined by McEnally and Kim as the "system of principles, policies, procedures, and clearly defined responsibilities and accountabilities used by stakeholders to overcome conflicts of interest inherent in the corporate form." Note that conflicts of interest are most severe in corporations because of the separation of ownership and management (versus sole proprietorship or partnership), so the focus is on corporate governance in primarily corporations.

An *agency relationship* occurs when an individual, who is referred to as the "agent," acts on behalf of another individual, who is referred to as the "principal." Such a relationship creates the potential for a principal-agent problem where the agent may act for his own well-being rather than that of the principal. Corporate governance systems are primarily concerned with potential principal-agent problems in two areas: (1) between managers and shareholders, and (2) between directors and shareholders.

Examples of ways that management may act for its own interests rather than those of shareholders include the following:

- Expanding the size of the firm for the benefit of management, not shareholder value.
- Granting excessive compensation and perquisites.
- Investing in ventures with returns too small to justify the risk.
- Not taking enough risk.

The following are guidelines for corporate governance best practices to remember for the exam:

- 75% of board members are independent.
- CEO and chairman are separate positions.
- Directors are knowledgeable and experienced and serve on only two or three boards.
- The board holds annual elections (not staggered elections).
- The board is annually evaluated and assessed.
- Board members meet annually without management present.
- The finance committee includes only independent directors with finance expertise, and the committee meets annually with auditors.
- Only independent directors serve on the nominating committee.
- Most of senior management's compensation is tied to performance.
- The board uses independent and outside counsel.
- The board is required to approve any related-party transactions.

The key is to remember the link between valuation and corporate governance. Empirical studies show that:

- Strong corporate governance increases profitability and shareholder returns.
- Weak corporate governance decreases company value by increasing risk to shareholders.

MERGERS AND ACQUISITIONS
Cross-Reference to CFA Institute Assigned Topic Review #28

Categorization

- *Statutory merger.* The target ceases to exist and all assets and liabilities become part of the acquirer.
- *Subsidiary merger.* The target company becomes a subsidiary of the acquirer.
- *Consolidations.* Both companies cease to exist in their prior form and come together to form a new company.

Types

- *Horizontal mergers.* Firms in similar lines of business combine.
- *Vertical mergers.* Combine firms either further up or down the supply chain.
- *Conglomerate mergers.* Combine firms in unrelated businesses.

Motivations

Common motivations behind M&A activity include the following:

- Achieving synergies.
- Growing more rapidly.
- Increasing market power.
- Gaining access to unique capabilities.
- Diversifying.
- Gaining personal benefits for managers.
- Taking advantage of tax benefits.
- Unlocking hidden value for a struggling company.
- Achieving international business goals.
- Bootstrapping earnings.

Bootstrapping is a technique whereby a high P/E firm acquires a low P/E firm in an exchange of stock. The total earnings of the combined firm are unchanged, but the total shares outstanding are less than the two separate entities. The result is higher reported earnings per share, even though there may be no economic gains.

Motivations and Industry Life Cycles

Figure 5: Merger Motivations in the Industry Life Cycle

Industry Life Cycle Stage	Industry Characteristics	Merger Motivation	Common Types of Mergers
Pioneer/ development	• Unsure of product acceptance • Large capital requirements and low profit margins	• Gain access to capital from more mature businesses • Share management talent	• Conglomerate • Horizontal
Rapid growth	• High profit margins • Accelerating sales and earnings • Competition still low	• Gain access to capital • Expand capacity to grow	• Conglomerate • Horizontal
Mature growth	• Lots of new competition • Still opportunities for above average growth	• Increase operational efficiencies • Economies of scale/synergies	• Horizontal • Vertical
Stabilization	• Competition has reduced growth potential • Capacity constraints	• Economies of scale/reduce costs • Improve management	• Horizontal
Decline	• Consumer tastes have shifted • Overcapacity/ shrinking profit margins	• Survival • Operational efficiencies • Acquire new growth opportunities	• Horizontal • Vertical • Conglomerate

Transaction Characteristics

- *Stock purchase.* The target's shareholders receive cash or shares of the acquiring company's stock in exchange for their shares of the target.
- *Asset purchase.* The payment is made directly to the target company in return for specific assets.

Figure 6: Key Differences Between Forms of Acquisition

	Stock Purchase	*Asset Purchase*
Payment	Made directly to target company shareholders in exchange for their shares	Made directly to target company
Approval	Majority shareholder approval required	No shareholder approval needed unless asset sale is substantial
Corporate taxes	None	Target company pays capital gains taxes
Shareholder taxes	Shareholders pay capital gains tax	None
Liabilities	Acquirer assumes liabilities of target	Acquirer usually avoids assumption of target's liabilities

Method of Payment

The method of payment in a merger transaction may be cash, stock, or a combination of the two. Cash offerings are straight forward, but in a stock offering, the exchange ratio determines the number of the acquirer's shares that each target company shareholder will receive.

When an acquirer is negotiating with a target over the method of payment, there are three main factors that should be considered:

1. Distribution between risk and reward for the acquirer and target shareholders.
2. Relative valuations of companies involved.
3. Changes in capital structure.

Attitude of Target Management

In a friendly merger, the acquirer and target work together to perform due diligence and sign a definitive merger agreement before submitting the merger proposal to the target's shareholders.

In a hostile merger, the acquirer seeks to avoid the target's management through a tender offer or proxy battle. If the target company's management does not support the deal, the acquirer submits a merger proposal directly to the target's board of directors in a process called *bear hug*. If the bear hug is unsuccessful, the next step is to appeal directly to the target's shareholders using one of two methods—a tender offer or a proxy battle.

1. In a *tender offer*, the acquirer offers to buy the shares directly from the target shareholders, and each individual shareholder either accepts or rejects the offer.

2. In a *proxy battle*, the acquirer seeks to control the target by having shareholders approve a new "acquirer approved" board of directors. A proxy solicitation is approved by regulators and then sent to the target's shareholders.

Takeover Defense Mechanisms

Pre-offer defense mechanisms:

- Poison pills.
- Poison puts.
- Reincorporating in a state with restrictive takeover laws.
- Staggered board elections.
- Restricted voting rights.
- Supermajority voting.
- Fair price amendments.
- Golden parachutes.

Post-offer defense mechanisms:

- "Just say no" defense.
- Litigation, greenmail.
- Share repurchases.
- Leveraged recapitalizations.
- "Crown jewel" defense.
- "Pac man" defense.
- Finding a white knight or white squire.

Herfindahl-Hirschman Index (HHI)

$$HHI = \sum_{i=1}^{n}(MS_i \times 100)^2$$

Figure 7: HHI Concentration Level and Likelihood of Antitrust Action

Post-Merger HHI	Industry Concentration	Change in Pre- and Post-Merger HHI	Antitrust Action
Less than 1,000	Not concentrated	Any amount	No action
Between 1,000 and 1,800	Moderately concentrated	100 or more	Possible antitrust challenge
Greater than 1,800	Highly concentrated	50 or more	Antitrust challenge virtually certain

Valuing a Merger Target

Discounted Cash Flow

To calculate free cash flow (FCF) for a target company and estimate its value using DCF analysis, we can use the following steps:

Step 1: Determine which free cash flow model to use for the analysis.

Step 2: Develop pro forma financial estimates.

Step 3: Calculate free cash flows using the pro forma data.

Step 4: Discount free cash flows back to the present at the appropriate discount rate.

Step 5: Determine the terminal value and discount it back to the present.

Step 6: Add the discounted FCF values for the first stage and the terminal value to determine the value of the target firm.

Advantages:

- It is relatively easy to model any changes in the target company's cash flow that may occur after the merger.
- It is based on forecasts of fundamental conditions in the future rather than on current data.
- It is easy to customize.

Disadvantages:

- The model is difficult to apply when free cash flows are negative.
- Estimates of cash flows and earnings are highly subject to error, especially when those estimates are for time periods far in the future.
- Discount rate changes over time can have a large impact on the valuation estimate.
- Estimation error is a major concern since the majority of the estimated value for the target is based on the terminal value, which is highly sensitive to estimates used for the constant growth rate and discount rate.

Comparable Company Analysis

Comparable company analysis uses relative valuation metrics for similar firms to determine a market value for the target, and then adds a takeover premium to this value.

Step 1: Identify the set of comparable firms.

Step 2: Calculate various relative value measures based on the current market prices of companies in the sample.

Step 3: Calculate descriptive statistics for the relative value metrics and apply those measures to the target firm.

Step 4: Estimate a takeover premium.

Step 5: Calculate the estimated takeover price for the target as the sum of estimated stock value based on comparables and the takeover premium.

Advantages:

- Data for comparable companies is easy to access.
- Assumption that similar assets should have similar values is fundamentally sound.
- Estimates of value are derived directly from the market rather than assumptions and estimates about the future.

Disadvantages:

- The approach implicitly assumes that the market's valuation of the comparable companies is accurate.
- Using comparable companies provides an estimate of a fair stock price, but not a fair takeover price. An appropriate takeover premium must be determined separately.
- It is difficult to incorporate merger synergies or changing capital structures into the analysis.
- Historical data used to estimate a takeover premium may not be timely, and therefore may not reflect current conditions in the M&A market.

Comparable Transaction Analysis

Comparable transaction analysis uses relative valuation metrics from recent takeover transactions so there is no need to calculate a separate takeover premium.

Step 1: Identify a set of recent takeover transactions.

Step 2: Calculate various relative value measures based on completed deal prices for the companies in the sample.

Step 3: Calculate descriptive statistics for the relative value metrics and apply those measures to the target firm.

Advantages:

- Since the approach uses data from actual transactions, there is no need to estimate a separate takeover premium.
- Estimates of value are derived directly from recent prices for actual deals completed in the marketplace rather than from assumptions and estimates about the future.
- Use of prices established by recent transactions reduces the risk that the target's shareholders could file a lawsuit against the target's managers and board of directors for mispricing the deal.

Disadvantages:

- The approach implicitly assumes that the M&A market valued past transactions accurately. If past transactions were over or underpriced, the mispricings will be carried over to the estimated value for the target.
- There may not be enough comparable transactions to develop a reliable data set for use in calculating the estimated target value. If the analyst isn't able to find enough similar companies, she may try to use M&A deals from other industries that are not similar enough to the deal being considered.
- It is difficult to incorporate merger synergies or changing capital structures into the analysis.

Evaluating a Merger Bid

Post-merger valuation for an acquirer: $V_{AT} = V_A + V_T + S - C$

 Professor's Note: The pre-merger value of the target should be the price of the target stock before any market speculation causes the target's stock prices to jump.

Gains accrued to the target: $gain_T = TP = P_T - V_T$

Gains accrued to the acquirer: $gain_A = S - TP = S - (P_T - V_T)$

With a cash offer, the target firm's shareholders will profit by the amount paid over its current share price (i.e., the takeover premium). However, this gain is capped at that amount. *With a stock offer,* the gains will be determined in part by the value of the combined firm, because the target firm's shareholders do not receive cash and just walk away, but rather retain ownership in the new firm. Accordingly, for a stock deal we must adjust our formula for the price of the target: $P_T = (N \times P_{AT})$.

Effect of Price and Payment Method

The *acquirer will want to pay the lowest* possible price (the premerger value of the target, V_T), while the *target wants to receive the highest* possible price (the premerger value of the target plus the expected synergies, $V_T + S$).

In a *cash offer*, the acquirer assumes the risk and receives the potential reward from the merger, while the gain for the target shareholders is limited to the takeover premium. If an acquirer makes a cash offer in a deal, but the synergies realized are greater than expected, the takeover premium for the target would remain unchanged while the acquirer reaps the additional reward. Likewise, if synergies were less than expected, the target would still receive the same takeover premium, but the acquirer's gain may evaporate.

In a *stock offer*, some of the risks and potential rewards from the merger shift to the target firm. When the target receives stock as payment, the target's shareholders become a part owner of the acquiring company. This means that if estimates of the potential synergies are wrong, the target will share in the upside if the actual synergies exceed expectations, but will also share in the downside if the actual synergies are below expectations.

The more confident both parties are that synergies will be realized, the more the acquirer will prefer to pay cash and the more the target will prefer to receive stock.

Types of Restructuring

- *Cash divestitures* involve a direct sale of a division to an outside party in exchange for cash.
- *Equity carve-outs* create a new independent company by giving a proportionate equity interest in a subsidiary to outside shareholders through a public offering of stock.
- *Spin-offs* create a new independent company by distributing shares to existing shareholders of the parent company.
- *Split-offs* allow shareholders to receive new shares of a division of the parent company by exchanging a portion of their parent company shares.
- *Liquidations* break up the firm and sell its assets piece by piece. Most liquidations are associated with bankruptcy.

Voluntary Divestitures

The reasons why a company may divest assets include the following:

- A division no longer fitting into management's strategy.
- Poor profitability for a division.
- Reverse synergy.
- To receive an infusion of cash.

EQUITY

Topic Weight on Exam	15–25%
SchweserNotes^{TM} Reference	Book 3, Pages 9–307

EQUITY VALUATION: APPLICATIONS AND PROCESS
Cross-Reference to CFA Institute Assigned Topic Review #29

Intrinsic value is the estimate of an asset's value that would be made by someone who has complete understanding of the characteristics of the asset and its issuing firm. To the extent that market prices are not perfectly (informationally) efficient, they may diverge from intrinsic values. The difference between an analyst's estimate of a security's intrinsic value and its market price has two components—the difference between the security's *actual* intrinsic value and its market price, and the difference between the security's actual intrinsic value and the analyst's estimate of the intrinsic value:

$$IV_{analyst} - price = (IV_{actual} - price) + (IV_{analyst} - IV_{actual})$$

The **going concern assumption** is simply the assumption that a company will continue to operate as a business (as opposed to going out of business). **Liquidation value** is an estimate of what the assets of the firm would bring if sold separately, net of the company's liabilities.

Equity valuation is the process of estimating the value of an asset by (1) using a model based on the variables the analyst believes determine the fundamental value of the asset or (2) comparing it to the observable market value of "similar" assets. Equity valuation models are used by analysts in a number of ways including stock selection, forecasting the value impact of corporate actions, providing fairness opinions, communication with analysts and investors, valuation of private firms, portfolio management, and asset allocation.

The **five elements of industry structure** that determine the competitive environment in which firms compete and drive successful competitive strategy (as developed by Professor Michael Porter) are:

1. Threat of new entrants in the industry.

2. Threat of substitutes.

3. Bargaining power of buyers.

4. Bargaining power of suppliers.

5. Rivalry among existing competitors.

The basic building blocks of equity valuation come from accounting information contained in the firm's reports and releases.

Quality of earnings issues can be broken down into several categories and may be addressed only in the footnotes and disclosures to the financial statements:

1. Accelerating or premature recognition of income.

2. Reclassifying gains and non-operating income.

3. Expense recognition and losses.

4. Amortization, depreciation, and discount rates.

5. Off-balance-sheet issues.

An **absolute valuation model** refers to one which estimates intrinsic value based on future earnings, cash flows, and risk. Dividend discount and free cash flow valuation models are examples of absolute valuation models.

A **relative valuation model** estimates the value of a security relative to market prices of other similar securities. Valuation based on price-to-earnings, price-to-cash flow, and price-to sales ratios of other securities or securities indexes are examples of relative valuation models.

In **choosing a valuation model,** the analyst should consider the purpose of the analysis and the characteristics of the firm, including whether it pays dividends, the stability of its cash flows, how well its earnings growth can be estimated, and the nature of its assets.

RETURN CONCEPTS
Cross-Reference to CFA Institute Assigned Topic Review #30

Holding period return is the increase in price of an asset plus any cash flow received from that asset, divided by the initial price of the asset. The holding period can be any length. Usually, it is assumed the cash flow comes at the end of the period:

$$\text{holding period return} = r = \frac{P_1 - P_0 + CF_1}{P_0} = \frac{P_1 + CF_1}{P_0} - 1$$

An asset's required return is the minimum expected return an investor requires given the asset's characteristics.

If expected return is greater (less) than required return, the asset is undervalued (overvalued). The mispricing can lead to a return from convergence of price to intrinsic value.

The equity risk premium (called the market risk premium in the CAPM context) is the return over the risk-free rate that investors require for holding equity securities.

equity risk premium = required return on equity index − risk-free rate

A historical estimate of the equity risk premium consists of the difference between the mean return on a broad-based, equity-market index and the mean return on U.S. Treasury bills over a given time period.

There are four types of estimates of the equity risk premium: (1) historical estimates, (2) forward-looking estimates, (3) macroeconomic model estimates, and (4) survey estimates.

1. The historical estimates are straightforward to compute, but they are not current.

2. Forward-looking estimates use current information, but that information needs to be updated periodically as new estimates are generated.

3. Macroeconomic models use current information, but they are only appropriate for developed countries where public equities represent a relatively large share of the economy.

4. Survey estimates are easy to obtain, but there can be a wide disparity between opinions.

Models used to estimate the equity risk premium:

- Gordon growth model:

$$(D_1 / P) + \hat{g} - r_{LT,0}$$

- Ibbotsen-Chen (supply side)

$$\text{equity risk premium} = [1 + \hat{i}] \times [1 + \widehat{rEg}] \times [1 + \widehat{PEg}] - 1 + \hat{Y} - \widehat{RF}$$

Models used to estimate the required return on equity:

- CAPM:

  required return on stock j = risk-free return + (equity risk premium) × (beta of j)

- Multifactor model:

  $$\text{required return} = RF + (\text{risk premium})_1 + \ldots + (\text{risk premium})_n$$

- Fama-French model:

$$\text{req. ret. of stock j} = RF + \beta_{mkt,j} \times (R_{mkt} - RF) + \beta_{SMB,j} \times (R_{small} - R_{big}) + \beta_{HML,j} \times (R_{HBM} - R_{LBM})$$

  where:
  $(R_{mkt} - RF)$ = market risk premium
  $(R_{small} - R_{big})$ = small-cap risk premium
  $(R_{HBM} - R_{LBM})$ = value risk premium

- The Pastor-Stambaugh model adds a liquidity factor to the Fama-French model.
- Macroeconomic multifactor models use factors associated with economic variables that would affect the cash flows and/or discount rate of companies.
- The build-up method is similar to the risk premium approach. One difference is that this approach does not use betas to adjust for the exposure to a factor. The bond yield plus risk premium method is a type of build-up method.

Beta estimation:

- A regression of the returns of a publicly-traded company's stock returns on the returns of an index provides an estimate of beta. For forecasting required returns using the CAPM, an analyst may wish to adjust for beta drift using the Blume method:

  adjusted beta = (2/3) × (regression beta) + (1/3) × (1.0)

- For thinly-traded stocks and non-publicly traded companies, an analyst can estimate beta using a four-step process: (1) identify publicly traded benchmark company; (2) estimate the beta of the benchmark company; (3) unlever the benchmark company's beta; and (4) relever the beta using the capital structure of the thinly-traded/non-public company.

Each of the various methods of estimating the required return on an equity investment has strengths and weaknesses.

- The CAPM is simple but may have low explanatory power.
- Multifactor models have more explanatory power but are more complex and costly.
- Build-up models are simple and can apply to closely held companies, but they typically use historical values as estimates that may or may not be relevant to the current situation.

THE FIVE COMPETITIVE FORCES THAT SHAPE STRATEGY
Cross-Reference to CFA Institute Assigned Topic Review #31

This is important material which has been in the curriculum for many years. Analysis of a firm requires an understanding of the firm's competitive environment. Two central questions provide the basis for the firm's choice of a competitive strategy:

1. *Industry attractiveness.* Is the industry attractive in terms of long-term profitability potential?

2. *Competitive advantage.* What determines a firm's relative competitive position within an industry?

Porter's Five Forces

Five forces determine the industry's degree of competitiveness and long-term profit potential. Memorize them!

1. *Entry barriers* (or threat of new entrants) for new competitors are a function of economies of scale, product differentials, brand identity, capital requirements, access to distribution channels, government policy, and cost advantages.

2. The *threat of substitutes* is a function of relative price performance of substitutes, buyer propensity to substitute, and switching cost.

3. *Bargaining power of buyers* is a function of bargaining leverage and price sensitivity.

4. *Bargaining power of suppliers* is determined by differentiation of inputs, presence of substitute inputs, supplier concentration, importance of volume to the supplier, and threat of forward integration.

5. *Rivalry among existing competitors* is a function of industry growth, fixed costs, value added, product differences, brand identity, diversity of competitors, exit barriers, and informational complexity.

You should be able to read a short description of an industry and then discuss how each of these factors contributes to the long-term attractiveness (or profitability) of the industry. *Memorize the five forces!*

YOUR STRATEGY NEEDS A STRATEGY
Cross-Reference to CFA Institute Assigned Topic Review #32

An appropriate strategic planning process should be consistent with the predictability and malleability of the environment in which the business operates. **Predictability** defines how accurately and how far into the future a company can forecast factors such as industry demand, corporate performance, and market expectations. **Malleability** is defined as the extent to which a company and its competitors can influence these industry factors.

Figure 1: Strategy Formulation Styles

	Less Predictable	*More Predictable*
Less Malleable	Adaptive	Classical
More Malleable	Shaping	Visionary

The **classical** style entails identification of a company's unique abilities and resources and formulation of a plan to achieve the most favorable market position. The classical style typically involves multiple rounds of methodical planning using quantitative prediction tools to generate long-term forecasts.

An **adaptive** style requires that a company be able to react quickly to change and emphasizes flexibility over efficiency. Under an adaptive style, strategies must be closely linked to operational processes to capture signals for change and to minimize information loss.

A **shaping** style involves influencing the unpredictable business environment to further the company's business interests. This can be achieved by:

- Building a network of committed customers, suppliers, and partners.
- Defining new markets, technologies, and business practices.
- Promoting the company's interests through marketing, lobbying, and strategic partnerships.

A **visionary** style does not take the environment as given, but seeks to alter it to further the company's interests. Visionary styles entail high risk and can be profoundly disruptive, often involving a so-called "build it and they will come" approach.

INDUSTRY AND COMPANY ANALYSIS
Cross-Reference to CFA Institute Assigned Topic Review #33

Forecasting Revenues

Bottom-up analysis starts with analysis of an individual company or reportable segments of a company. **Top-down analysis** begins with expectations about a macroeconomic variable, often the expected growth rate of nominal GDP. A **hybrid analysis** incorporates elements of both top-down and bottom-up analysis.

When forecasting revenue with a *growth relative to GDP growth approach*, the relationship between GDP and company sales is estimated, and then company sales growth is forecast based on an estimate for future GDP growth. The *market growth and market share approach* begins with an estimate of industry sales (market growth), and then company sales are estimated as a percentage (market share) of industry sales. Forecast revenue then equals the forecasted market size multiplied by the forecasted market share.

Forecasting Expenses

COGS is primarily a variable cost and is often modeled as a percentage of estimated future revenue. Expectations of changes in input prices can be used to improve COGS estimates. The R&D and corporate overhead components of SG&A are likely to be stable over the short term, while selling and distribution costs will tend to increase with increases in sales.

A company with **economies of scale** will have lower costs and higher operating margins as production volume increases and should exhibit positive correlation between sales volume and margins. Economies of scale in an industry are evidenced by the existence of lower costs (proportional to revenues) for larger companies in an industry as compared to their smaller peers.

Increases in input costs will increase COGS unless a company has hedged the risk of input price increases with derivatives or contracts for future delivery. Vertically integrated companies are likely to be less affected by increasing input costs. The effect on sales of increasing product prices to reflect higher COGS will depend on the elasticity of demand for the products and on the timing and amount of competitors' price increases.

Some advances in technology decrease costs of production, which will increase profit margins (at least for early adopters). Other advances in technology will result in either improved substitutes or wholly new products. One way for an analyst to model the introduction of new substitutes for a company's products is to estimate a **cannibalization factor**—the percentage of the market for the existing product that will be taken by the new substitute.

The primary determinants of gross interest expense are the amount of debt outstanding (gross debt) and interest rates. Net interest expense is gross interest expense minus interest income on cash and short-term debt securities owned.

Forecasting Balance Sheet Items

Certain balance sheet items (e.g., accounts receivable, inventory, accounts payable) can be estimated based on their historical relationships with income statement items. Property, plant, and equipment (PP&E) forecasts may be improved by analyzing capital expenditures for maintenance separately from capital expenditures for growth.

Return on Invested Capital (ROIC)

Forecasts resulting in higher ROIC than a firm's peers can be the result of a competitive advantage, a favorable force (from Porter's five force analysis), or inappropriate historical financial data having been used as a basis for the forecast.

Estimating Long-Term Growth Rate

Terminal value estimates are very sensitive to estimates of long-term growth rate. Analysts should be on the lookout for **inflection points**: times when growth trajectory is expected to change significantly.

DISCOUNTED DIVIDEND VALUATION
Cross-Reference to CFA Institute Assigned Topic Review #34

DCF METHODS

Discounted cash flow (DCF) valuation is based on the idea that the value today of any security is the discounted value of all future cash flows.

Dividend discount models (DDMs). The DDM defines cash flow as dividends to be received in the future. This is based on the idea that, over time, earnings and dividends will converge. The DDM is most appropriate for mature and profitable firms that are not engaged in a fast-growing segment of the economy, or for large, diversified portfolios like the S&P 500. Use the DDM for valuation problems with the following characteristics:

- The firm has a dividend history.
- The dividend policy is consistent and related to earnings.
- The perspective is that of a minority shareholder.

Free cash flow (FCF) *models.* Cash flow from a security can also be defined as free cash flow. Two versions of FCF valuation exist: FCF to the firm (FCFF) and FCF to equity (FCFE). FCFF is the cash flow generated by the firm above that required to be reinvested to maintain current operations. FCFE is FCFF minus debt service and preferred dividends. FCF valuation is appropriate when the following characteristics exist:

- The firm does not have a stable dividend policy.
- The firm has a dividend policy that is not related to earnings.
- The firm's FCF is related to profitability.
- The perspective is that of a controlling shareholder.

Residual income (RI). Residual income refers to the amount of earnings during the period that exceed the investor's required earnings. Think of residual income as *economic profit.* In this framework, the value of the firm's equity is the firm's book value plus the present value of all future residual income. The RI method can be difficult to apply because it requires an in-depth analysis of the firm's accounting accruals.

The RI method is most appropriate under the following conditions:

- The firm does not have a dividend history.
- The firm's FCF is negative.
- It is a firm with transparent and high quality accounting.

In all cases, you will have to forecast the future cash flows (dividends, free cash flow, or residual income), determine the appropriate discount rate, and discount the cash flows to obtain the value of the firm. For the DDM, FCFE, and RI methods, the appropriate discount rate is the cost of equity. In general, there are three methods for determining the cost of equity:

1. The CAPM:

$$E(r) = r_f + \{\beta \times [E(r_m) - r_f]\}$$

2. Multifactor models such as the Arbitrage Pricing Theory or the Fama French Model.

3. The build-up method, such as adding a risk premium to the firm's bond yield.

For the FCFF model, the appropriate discount rate is the weighted average cost of capital (WACC).

Now let's turn to the specifics of the valuation methods.

There are four versions of the multiperiod DDM: (1) the Gordon growth model, (2) 2-stage growth model, (3) H-model, and (4) 3-stage growth model. We will review only the first three, since the 3-stage model is an extension of the 2-stage version.

Gordon Growth Model

The *Gordon growth model* assumes that dividends will grow at a constant rate forever. The formula is as follows:

$$V_0 = \frac{D_0(1+g)}{r-g} = \frac{D_1}{r-g}$$

The constant growth rate in dividends and earnings is *g*. Note that the value today, V_0, is dependent on the amount of the dividend one period from today, D_1. The model also assumes that *r* is greater than *g*. You can solve the Gordon model for either *r* or *g* to determine the required return or growth rate implicit in the current market price.

 Professor's Note: If you're using the Gordon model on the exam, make sure you have next year's dividend, D_1. If you are given the current dividend, D_0, you can get next year's dividend as: $D_1 = D_0 \times (1+g)$.

A related construct is the *present value of growth opportunities* (PVGO). This simply says that the value of the stock today is equal to its nongrowth value (E_1 / r) plus the PVGO:

$$V_0 = \frac{E_1}{r} + PVGO$$

The main use of this idea is to plug in the current market price as V_0 and calculate the PVGO implied in the market price (large PVGO indicates high expected growth).

The Gordon growth model is most appropriate for mature, stable firms. The limitations of the Gordon model include the following:

- Valuations are very sensitive to estimates of r and g.
- The model assumes that the firm is paying dividends now, or will be during the foreseeable future.
- Unpredictable growth patterns from some firms make using the model difficult.

Two-Stage Growth Model

The multistage models are somewhat more complex. Basically, the multistage models (e.g., the 2-stage growth model and the H-model) *assume that there is some temporary short-term growth period followed by a stable long-term growth period.* The 2-stage model normally assumes that the firm will experience a high rate of growth for the next few years followed by low growth for eternity.

The value of the stock is the present value of the dividends during the high-growth period plus the present value of the terminal value. The terminal value can be estimated using the Gordon growth model or a market multiple approach.

H-Model

The H-model assumes that growth is currently high, but decreases at a linear rate toward the low-growth rate. Once the low-growth rate is reached, the H-model assumes that the low-growth rate will prevail forever. The difference between the two models is how the growth rate changes from high growth to low growth. The 2-stage model assumes that the change happens at one point in time. The H-model assumes that the growth rate declines in a linear fashion from the current (high) growth rate to the long-term (stable) growth rate over t years.

The approximate value of a firm's equity using the H-model is:

$$V_0 = \frac{D_0 \times \left(1 + g_L\right)}{r - g_L} + \frac{D_0 \times H \times \left(g_S - g_L\right)}{r - g_L}$$

where:

$H = \left(\dfrac{t}{2}\right)$ = half-life (in years) of high-growth period

t = length of high-growth period

g_S = short-term growth rate

g_L = long-term growth rate

r = required return

Note that the second term is the value of growth in excess of g_L and that the first is the value of the firm with constant growth of g_L.

Solving for Required Return

You can use any of the models to solve for the required rate of return given the other model inputs. For the multistage models, the algebra gets complex and is very unlikely to show up on the exam.

For the Gordon (or stable growth) model, solving for return yields:

$$r = \frac{D_1}{P_0} + g$$

This is a handy tool for backing into the required rate of return.

The Sustainable Growth Rate

The *sustainable growth rate* (SGR) is defined as the rate that earnings (and dividends) can continue to grow indefinitely, given that a firm's capital structure is unchanged and it doesn't issue any new equity. SGR can be derived from the relationship between the firm's retention rate and ROE as determined by the DuPont formula:

$$g = \left(\frac{\text{net income} - \text{dividends}}{\text{net income}}\right) \times \left(\frac{\text{net income}}{\text{sales}}\right)$$
$$\times \left(\frac{\text{sales}}{\text{total assets}}\right) \times \left(\frac{\text{total assets}}{\text{stockholders' equity}}\right)$$

This has also been called the *PRAT model*, where SGR is a function of the profit margin (P), the retention rate (R), the asset turnover (A), and the degree of financial leverage (T). Unless otherwise instructed on the exam, use beginning-of-period balance sheet value to calculate SGR and to construct the DuPont model.

FREE CASH FLOW VALUATION
Cross-Reference to CFA Institute Assigned Topic Review #35

Free cash flow to the firm (FCFF) is the cash available to all of the firm's investors, including common stockholders, preferred stockholders, and bondholders after the firm buys and sells products, provides services, pays its cash operating expenses, and makes short- and long-term investments. *Free cash flow to equity* (FCFE) is the cash available to the common stockholders after funding capital requirements, working capital needs, and debt financing requirements.

The FCFE/FCFF framework is analogous to the DDM framework. The main difference is that now we must be very careful to correctly calculate FCFF and FCFE from the income statement or the statement of cash flows, and we must make sure that we are using the correct discount rate (use the equity cost of capital with FCFE and the WACC with the FCFF).

Use the FCF model instead of DDM if the following conditions apply:

- The firm does not pay cash dividends.
- Dividend policy does not reflect the firm's long-run profitability.
- The firm is a take-over target (because FCF models take a control perspective).

Free Cash Flow to the Firm

There are four definitions for FCFF depending on the data given. Unfortunately, we are going to advise you to know all four (if that's just too much, then you should concentrate on the first and the last). Assuming that the only noncash charge is depreciation, the four definitions are as follows:

FCFF from NI: FCFF = NI + dep + [interest × (1 − tax rate)] − FCInv − WCInv

FCFF from EBIT: FCFF = [EBIT × (1 − tax rate)] + dep − FCInv − WCInv

FCFF from EBITDA:
FCFF = [EBITDA × (1 − tax rate)] + (dep × tax rate) − FCInv − WCInv

FCFF from CFO: FCFF = CFO + [interest × (1 − tax rate)] − FCInv

where:
FCInv   = net investment in fixed capital (commonly called capex)
WCInv = net investment in working capital (excluding cash)
EBITDA = earnings before interest, taxes, depreciation, and amortization

Free Cash Flow to Equity

We have four formulas for calculating FCFE:

FCFE from FCFF: FCFE = FCFF − [interest × (1 − tax rate)] + net borrowing

FCFE from NI: FCFE = NI + dep − FCInv − WCInv + net borrowing

FCFE from CFO: FCFE = CFO − FCInv + net borrowing

FCFE with target debt ratio:
FCFE = NI − [(1 − DR) × (FCInv − dep)] − [(1 − DR) × WCInv]

In the last version, DR stands for the constant debt ratio. It is *imperative* that you know how to calculate FCFF and FCFE. This looks like a formidable task (and it is), but if you look at the accounting relationships you'll see that there is a lot of overlap between the formulas. Also, note that you use these formulas to calculate FCFF and FCFE given the accounting inputs.

Dividends, share repurchases, and share issues have no effect on FCFF and FCFE; leverage changes have only a minor effect on FCFE and no effect on FCFF.

Single-Stage FCFF/FCFE Models

Valuation using FCFF and FCFE is very similar to valuation using the DDMs. Let's begin with single-stage valuation. The formulas (which should look familiar) are as follows:

For FCFF valuation: firm value $= \dfrac{FCFF_1}{WACC - g}$

For FCFE valuation: equity value $= \dfrac{FCFE_1}{\text{required return on equity} - g}$

Note that to find the value of the firm today, the numerator is next year's FCF (i.e., $FCFF_1$ and $FCFE_1$). *It is imperative that you use the correct discount rate with the correct formula.* Since the FCFF framework values the entire firm, the cost of capital from all sources must be used (i.e., WACC). FCFE values only the cash flows that belong to equity holders; hence, the equity discount rate, *r*, is appropriate (think CAPM).

Two-Stage FCFF/FCFE Models

The 2-stage FCF framework is also analogous to the 2-stage DDM framework.

Remember the following steps:

Step 1: Chart the FCFs in high-growth period.
Step 2: Use single-stage FCF model to calculate terminal value at end of high-growth period.
Step 3: Discount interim FCF and terminal value to time zero to find value; use WACC with FCFF to find firm value; use required return on equity with FCFE to find equity value.

 Professor's Note: The guiding principle behind DCF valuation is that the value of the security is simply the discounted value of all future cash flows.

MARKET-BASED VALUATION: PRICE MULTIPLES
Cross-Reference to CFA Institute Assigned Topic Review #36

Price multiples are ratios of a common stock's market price to some fundamental variable. The most common example is the price-to-earnings (P/E) ratio. A **justified price multiple** is what the multiple *should be* if the stock is fairly valued. If the actual multiple is greater than the justified price multiple, the stock is overvalued; if the actual multiple is less than the justified multiple, the stock is undervalued (all else equal).

A price multiple can be justified based on one of two methods:

1. The justified price multiple for the **method of comparables** is an average multiple of similar stocks in the same peer group. The economic rationale for the method of comparables is the Law of One Price, which asserts that two similar assets should sell at comparable prices (i.e., multiples).

2. The justified price multiple for the **method of forecasted fundamentals** is the ratio of the value of the stock from a discounted cash flow (DCF) valuation model divided by some fundamental variable (e.g., earnings per share). The economic rationale for the method of forecasted fundamentals is that the value used in the numerator of the justified price multiple is derived from a DCF model that is based on the most basic concept in finance: value is equal to the present value of expected future cash flows discounted at the appropriate risk-adjusted rate of return.

The Price-to-Earnings (P/E) Ratio

The most common market multiple is the P/E ratio. The main argument in favor of P/E valuation is that earnings power, as measured by EPS, is the primary determinant of investment value. There are a few problems with using the P/E ratio as a valuation tool:

- Earnings can be negative, which makes the P/E meaningless.
- The volatile, transitory portion of earnings makes the interpretation of P/Es difficult for analysts.
- Management has considerable discretion over accounting choices that affect reported earnings.

The P/E ratio can be calculated on a *leading* or *trailing basis*. On a trailing basis, earnings over the last 12 months are used in the denominator. With a leading basis, next year's expected earnings are used in the denominator.

While the price is always the market price of a share of stock, the analyst must determine the EPS. Analysts frequently use normalized EPS rather than EPS from the most recent financial statements. There are two methods of normalization:

1. *Historical average EPS.* The EPS in the P/E ratio is the historical average from the most recent complete business cycle.

2. *Average ROE.* The EPS in the P/E ratio is the average ROE over the most recent complete business cycle times the current book value per share.

On the exam, you are most likely to be presented with a market multiple valuation question dealing with forecasted fundamentals (as opposed to the comparison sample method). In all cases we present here, *the "forecasted fundamentals method" is economics-talk for rearranging the DCF formulas to solve for the desired market-multiple relationship.* In most cases, this involves rearranging (and substituting into) the Gordon model. For the P/E ratio, if you substitute and rearrange, you get the formulas for the forecasted fundamental P/E ratio:

$$\text{justified leading P/E} = \frac{P_0}{E_1} = \frac{1-b}{r-g}$$

$$\text{justified trailing P/E} = \frac{P_0}{E_0} = \frac{(1-b)(1+g)}{r-g}$$

In both formulas, *b* is the retention ratio [so (1 − b) is the payout ratio]. You should be able to determine how changes in the variables in the formula impact the justified P/E. All else equal, the higher the required rate of return, the lower the P/E will be; the higher the growth rate, the higher the P/E will be.

The PEG Ratio

The PEG ratio is equal to the ratio of the P/E multiple to earnings growth:

$$\text{PEG ratio} = \frac{\text{P/E}}{\text{g}}$$

The implied valuation rule is that stocks with lower PEG ratios are undervalued relative to high-PEG stocks, assuming similar risk.

The Price-to-Book (P/B) Ratio

The P/B ratio is calculated as the market price per share divided by the book value per share (common stockholders' equity = total assets − total liabilities − preferred stock). The *advantages* of the P/B ratio include the following:

- Book value is usually positive, even when earnings are negative.
- Book value is more stable than EPS.
- Book value is an appropriate measure of net asset value (especially for firms such as financial institutions that hold liquid assets).

The *disadvantages* of the P/B ratio include the following:

- P/Bs can be misleading when there are significant size differences between firms.
- Book value is influenced by accounting choices/conventions.
- Inflation and technology can cause the book value and the market value of assets to differ significantly.

As with the P/E ratio, if we substitute into and rearrange the Gordon model, we can obtain a formula for the justified P/B:

$$\text{justified P/B} = \frac{\text{ROE} - \text{g}}{\text{r} - \text{g}}$$

The P/B increases as ROE increases. It also increases as the spread between ROE and *r* increases. Common adjustments to the book value include the exclusion of intangible assets such as goodwill. Since the book value forecasts are not widely disseminated like EPS forecasts, analysts typically use trailing book value when calculating P/Bs.

The Price-to-Sales (P/S) Ratio

The P/S ratio is calculated by dividing the firm's stock price by revenue per share. The *advantages* of the P/S ratio include the following:

- The ratio is meaningful even for distressed firms.
- Sales revenue is not easily manipulated.
- P/S ratios are not as volatile as P/E ratios.
- P/S ratios are particularly useful in valuing mature, cyclical, and zero-income (start-up) firms.

The *disadvantages* of using the P/S ratio include the following:

- High sales do not necessarily mean high profits or cash flows.
- The P/S ratio does not capture differences in the cost structure between firms.
- Revenue recognition practices still distort sales.

Allowing PM_0 to denote the trailing profit margin (defined as NI/sales), we can substitute into and rearrange the Gordon model to get the formula for the justified P/S ratio:

$$\text{justified P/S ratio} = \frac{\left(E_0 \big/ S_0\right) \times (1-b) \times (1+g)}{r-g}$$

$$= \text{net profit margin} \times \text{justified trailing P/E}$$

The P/S increases as the profit margin increases and as growth increases. The P/S ratio is usually calculated using trailing sales.

Price-to-Cash-Flow Ratios

Since value depends largely on the ability of the firm to generate cash, price-to-cash-flow multiples make intuitive sense. The *advantages* of using price-to-cash-flow multiples include the following:

- Cash flow is more difficult for managers to manipulate.
- Price-to-cash-flow is more stable than P/E.
- Price-to-cash-flow mitigates many concerns about the quality of reported earnings.

The *disadvantages* of price-to-cash-flow multiples include the following:

- Determining true cash flow from operations may be difficult.
- FCFE may be better than cash flow to the entire firm, but it's also more volatile.

But which measure of cash flow do we use? There are several cash flow measures with which you should be familiar:

- *Price-to-cash-flow (P/CF):* CF = NI + depreciation + amortization.
- *Price-to-adjusted CFO (P/CFO):* adjusted CFO = CFO + [(net cash interest outflow) × (1 − tax rate)].
- *Price-to-FCFE:* FCFE = CFO − FCInv + net borrowing.
- *Price-to-EBITDA:* EBITDA = earnings before interest, taxes, depreciation, and amortization.

Theoretically, FCFE is the preferred way to define cash flow. However, FCFE is also more volatile than traditional cash flow. EBITDA is a measure of cash flow to all providers of capital (i.e., both debt and equity). Hence, it may be better suited to valuing the entire firm rather than just the equity stake. Analysts typically use trailing cash flows when calculating price-to-cash-flow ratios.

Methods of Comparables

The basic idea of the method of comparables is to compare a stock's price multiple to the benchmark. *Firms with multiples below the benchmark are undervalued, and firms with multiples above the benchmark are overvalued.*

However, the fundamentals of the stock should be similar to the fundamentals of the benchmark before we can make direct comparisons and draw any conclusions about whether the stock is overvalued or undervalued. In other words, we have to ensure that we're comparing apples to apples (sorry for the cliché). That's why the fundamental variables (i.e., the fundamentals) that affect each multiple are important in applying the method of comparables.

RESIDUAL INCOME VALUATION
Cross-Reference to CFA Institute Assigned Topic Review #37

Residual income, or economic profit, is equal to the net income of a firm less a charge that measures stockholders' opportunity costs in generating that income. That is, residual income recognizes that accounting profits actually overstate economic profit since the cost of the capital committed to the firm is not included in the calculation of accounting profit (note the similarities to our discussion of EVA®). Residual income is calculated as follows:

RI = net income − equity charge

where:
equity charge = equity capital × cost of equity

Residual Income Model Valuation

The residual income model can be used in a valuation setting. Residual income breaks the firm value into two components:

1. Adjusted current book value of equity.

2. Present value of expected future RI.

Under the residual income model, the intrinsic value of the stock can be expressed as follows:

$$V_0 = B_0 + \left\{ \frac{RI_1}{(1+r)^1} + \frac{RI_2}{(1+r)^2} + \frac{RI_3}{(1+r)^3} + ... \right\}$$

where:
B_0 = current book value
RI_t = $E_t - (r \times B_{t-1}) = (ROE - r)(B_{t-1})$
r = required return on equity
ROE = expected return on new investments (expected return on equity)

The *single-stage residual income model* assumes residual income grows at a constant rate (g) which is less than the required return on equity (r).

$$V_0 = B_0 + \left[\frac{(ROE - r) \times B_0}{r - g} \right]$$

Strengths and Weaknesses of the Residual Income Approach

The *strengths* of the residual income approach include the following:

- Terminal value does not dominate the valuation equation (as with DDM and FCFE approaches).
- Residual income uses available accounting data.
- Residual income is applicable to non-dividend-paying firms.
- Residual income focuses on economic profits.

The *limitations* of the residual income approach are as follows:

- The accounting data may be manipulated by management.
- The accounting data may require significant adjustment.
- The model assumes a clean surplus relationship (i.e., ending BV = beginning BV + earnings – dividends).

The model is most appropriate for non-dividend paying firms, firms with negative FCF for the foreseeable future, or firms with high uncertainty about the terminal value of the equity.

Accounting Issues

There are many accounting issues associated with the residual income approach. Any accounting procedure that results in a direct charge to equity (e.g., foreign currency translation adjustments and some pension adjustments, etc.) will cause the residual income approach to break down. If the residual income model shows up on the exam, the most likely accounting issues that you will have to deal with involve balance sheet adjustments. Common balance sheet adjustments that you may have to allow for include the following:

- Changing inventory value from LIFO to current value.
- Capitalization of operating leases.
- Pension asset/liability issues.
- Goodwill.

On the exam, make the adjustments to the balance sheet and then calculate the value of the stock with the residual income method.

Multistage Residual Income Model

To implement a multistage residual income model, forecast residual income over a short-term, high-growth horizon (e.g., five years) and then make some simplifying assumptions about the pattern of residual income growth over the long term after the high-growth phase. *Continuing residual income* is the residual income that is expected over the long term. In the multistage residual income model, intrinsic value is the sum of three components:

$$V_0 = B_0 + \text{(PV of interim high-growth RI)} + \text{(PV of continuing residual income)}$$

Continuing residual income will continue beyond a specified earnings horizon depending on the fortunes of the industry, as well as on the sustainability of a specific firm's competitive prospects over the longer term. The projected rate at which residual income is expected to fade over the life cycle of the firm is captured by a persistence factor, which is between zero and one.

To simplify the model, we typically make one of the following assumptions about continuing residual income over the long term:

- Residual income is expected to persist at its current level forever.
- Residual income is expected to drop immediately to zero.

©2016 Kaplan, Inc.

- Residual income is expected to decline to a long-run average level consistent with a mature industry.
- Residual income is expected to decline over time as ROE falls to the cost of equity (in which case residual income is eventually zero).

An analysis of the firm's position in its industry and the structure of the industry will be necessary to justify one of these assumptions. The third scenario is the most realistic if we assume that over time industry competition reduces economic profits to the point at which firms begin to leave the industry and ROE stabilizes at a long-run normal level. The strength of the persistence factor will depend partly on the sustainability of the firm's competitive advantage and the structure of the industry: the more sustainable the competitive advantage and the better the industry prospects, the higher the persistence factor.

PRIVATE COMPANY VALUATION
Cross-Reference to CFA Institute Assigned Topic Review #38

Private firms include sole proprietorships and privately held corporations (not publicly traded). Valuation of private firms is based on some of the same company-specific factors which influence the value of publicly traded firms, such as:

- Stage of lifecycle.
- Firm size.
- Influence of short term investors.
- Quality and depth of management.
- Management/shareholder overlap.
- Quality of financial and other information.
- Taxes.

The stock of private firms, however, will typically have less liquidity and more restrictions on marketability than publicly traded shares. Private firms also typically have more concentrated ownership of its equity.

Reasons for Valuing the Total Capital of Private Companies

There are three primary reasons for valuing the total capital and/or equity capital of private companies: (1) transaction-related valuations, (2) compliance-related valuations, and (3) litigation-related valuations.

Transaction-related valuations are necessary when selling or financing a firm.

- Venture capital financing.
- Initial public offering (IPO).
- Sale in an acquisition.
- Bankruptcy proceedings.
- Performance-based managerial compensation.

Compliance-related valuations are performed for legal or regulatory reasons and primarily focus on financial reporting and tax issues.

Litigation-related valuations may be required for shareholder suits, damage claims, lost profits claims, or divorce settlements.

The appropriate valuation method depends on what the valuation will be used for and whether the firm is a going concern. Alternative **definitions of value** include:

- Fair market value.
- Fair value for financial reporting.
- Fair value for litigation.
- Market value.
- Investment value.
- Intrinsic value.

Approaches to Private Company Valuation

- *Income approach:* Values a firm as the present value of its expected future income. Such valuation has many valuations and may be based on a variety of different assumptions.
- *Market approach:* Values a firm using the price multiples based on recent sales of comparable assets.
- *Asset-based approach:* Values a firm's assets minus its liabilities.

Estimating Normalized Earnings

Normalized earnings should exclude nonrecurring and unusual items. In the case of private firms with a concentrated control, there may be discretionary or tax-motivated expenses, excessive compensation, or payment of personal expenses by the firm that require adjustment when estimating normalized earnings. Many analysts also adjust for company-owned real estate, removing the revenues and expenses of the real estate from the income statement and putting in a market-based estimate of rental cost of real estate used in the company's operations. The value of the real estate is then added to the income-based value of the firm as if owned real estate is all a non-operating asset of the firm. These adjustments can be quite significant when the firm is small.

Strategic and Nonstrategic Buyers

A transaction may be either strategic or financial (nonstrategic). In a strategic transaction, valuation of the firm is based in part on the perceived synergies of the target with the acquirer's other assets. A financial transaction assumes no synergies, as when one firm buys another in a dissimilar industry.

Discount Rate Estimation

Estimating the discount rate in a private firm valuation can be quite challenging for the following reasons.

- *Size premiums:* Size premiums are often added to the discount rates for small private companies. Estimating this premium using small public firm data may be biased upward by the fact many of the small firms in the sample are experiencing financial distress.
- *Availability and cost of debt:* A private firm may have less access to debt financing than a public firm. Because equity capital is usually more expensive than debt and because the higher operating risk of smaller private companies results in a higher cost of debt as well, WACC will typically be higher for private firms.
- *Acquirer versus target:* When acquiring a private firm, some acquirers will incorrectly use their own (lower) cost of capital, rather than the higher rate appropriate for the target, and arrive at a value for the target company that is too high.
- *Projection risk:* Because of the lower availability of information from private firms and managers who are inexperienced at forecasting, that analyst should increase the discount rate used.
- Management may not be experienced with forecasting and may underestimate or overestimate future earnings, requiring adjustment by the analyst. Such adjustments are highly subjective, however.
- *Lifecycle stage:* It is particularly difficult to estimate the discount rate for firms in an early stage of development. If such firms have unusually high levels of unsystematic risk, the use of the CAPM may be inappropriate. Although ranges of discount rates can be specified for the various lifecycle stages, it may difficult to classify the stage a firm is in.

CAPM Limitations

Using the CAPM, the expanded CAPM, and build-up methods to estimate discount rates for private firms may not be as straightforward as that for public firms.

- *CAPM:* Typically, beta is estimated from public firm data, and this may not be appropriate for private firms that have little chance of going public or being acquired by a public firm. Due to the differences between large public firms and small private firms, some U.S. tax courts have rejected the use of the CAPM for private firms.
- *Expanded CAPM:* This version of the CAPM includes additional premiums for size and firm-specific (unsystematic) risk.

- *Build-up method:* When it is not possible to find comparable public firms for beta estimation, the build-up method can be used. Beginning with the expected return on the market (beta is implicitly assumed to be one), premiums are added for small size, industry factors, and company specific factors.

Market Approaches to Valuation

- The *guideline public company method* uses the market values of similar publicly traded shares adjusted for differences in growth and risk between the two companies.
- The *guideline transactions method* uses the values from actual sales of controlling positions in either public or private companies.
- The *prior transaction method* uses sales prices from actual transactions in the subject company's shares.

Asset-Based Approaches to Valuation

The asset-based approach estimates the value of firm equity as the fair value of its assets minus the fair value of its liabilities. It is generally not used for going concerns.

Control and Marketability

A controlling equity position is regarded as more valuable than a minority position, as it gives the owner the ability to determine company strategy and dividend policy. Shares that are more marketable (liquid) are more valuable than otherwise identical, less marketable shares.

When estimating share values relative to market or transactions prices for similar shares, adjustment must be made for differences in control and marketability. For example, comparable values are for publicly traded shares, should be reduced by a discount for lack of marketability. The size of a marketability discount can be estimated using the difference between the sales price of traded shares and restricted shares of the same company or the difference between pre-IPO and post-IPO sales prices of shares.

On the other hand, if the comparable value is for publicly traded shares (a minority position) and the analyst is valuing a controlling interest in a private company, he would add a control premium to the comparable's value. Of course, if the comparable value is for a controlling position and the analyst is valuing a minority position, a discount for lack of control would be appropriate.

Alternative Investments

Topic Weight on Exam	5–10%
SchweserNotes™ Reference	Book 4, Pages 9–139

Private Real Estate Investments
Cross-Reference to CFA Institute Assigned Topic Review #39

Real Estate Investments

Figure 1 shows types of real estate investments.

Figure 1: Basic Forms of Real Estate Investment

	Debt	*Equity*
Private	Mortgages	Direct investments such as sole ownership, partnerships, and commingled funds
Public	Mortgage-backed securities	Shares of REITs and REOCs

Reasons to Invest in Real Estate and Risks of Investing

Reasons to invest in real estate include generation of current income and capital appreciation, as an inflation hedge, for portfolio diversification, and for tax benefits.

Principal risks of investing in real estate include the influence of business conditions on valuation, lead time in developing new property, cost and availability of capital, unexpected inflation, influence of demographic factors, lack of liquidity, environmental issues, lack of information, need for management expertise, and the use of leverage.

Real Estate Valuation

Appraisers use three different approaches to value real estate: the cost approach, the income approach, and the sales comparison approach.

1. The Cost Approach to Valuation

Under the *cost approach*, a value is derived by adding the value of the land to the current replacement cost of a new building less adjustments for estimated depreciation and obsolescence. The steps involved with applying the cost approach are:

1. Estimate the market value of the land.

2. Estimate the building's replacement cost.

3. Deduct depreciation including physical deterioration, functional obsolescence, locational obsolescence, and economic obsolescence.

The cost approach is most useful 1) when the subject property is relatively new, 2) for unusual properties, or 3) for properties where comparable transactions are limited.

2. The Income Approach to Valuation

The *income approach* includes two different valuation methods: the **direct capitalization method** and the **discounted cash flow method**. With the *direct capitalization method*, value is based on capitalizing the first-year net operating income (NOI) of the property using a *capitalization (cap) rate*. With the *discounted cash flow method*, value is based on the present value of the property's future cash flows using an appropriate discount rate.

Net operating income (NOI) is the amount of income remaining after subtracting vacancy and collection losses, as well as operating expenses such as insurance, property taxes, utilities, maintenance, and repairs, from potential gross income. NOI is calculated before subtracting financing costs and income taxes.

If the NOI and value are expected to grow at a constant rate, the cap rate is lower than the discount rate:

cap rate = discount rate − growth rate

Cap rate is used to capitalize first-year NOI as follows:

$$\text{value} = V_0 = \frac{NOI_1}{\text{cap rate}}$$

Cap rate can also be estimated from comparables:

$$\text{cap rate} = \frac{\text{NOI}_1}{\text{comparable sales price}}$$

Example: Valuation using the direct capitalization method

Suppose the net operating income of an office building is expected to be $175,000 and the cap rate is 8%. **Estimate** the market value of the property using the direct capitalization method.

Answer:

The estimated market value is:

$$V_0 = \frac{\text{NOI}_1}{\text{cap rate}} = \frac{\$175,000}{8\%} = \$2,187,500$$

The gross income multiplier, another form of direct capitalization, is the ratio of the sales price to the property's expected gross income in the year after purchase. The gross income multiplier can be derived from comparable transactions.

$$\text{gross income multiplier} = \frac{\text{sales price}}{\text{gross income}}$$

Once we obtain the gross income multiplier, value is estimated as a multiple of a subject property's estimated gross income as follows:

$$\text{value} = \text{gross income} \times \text{gross income multiplier}$$

Using the discounted cash flow (DCF) method, investors usually project NOI for a specific holding period, plus the property value at the end of the holding period (i.e., terminal value). Terminal value can be estimated by capitalizing future NOI at a future cap rate known as the *terminal* or *residual cap rate*. The terminal cap rate may be different from the *"going-in"* (initial) *cap rate*.

When tenants are required to pay all expenses, a cap rate may be applied to rent instead of to NOI. The cap rate that results from dividing rent by comparable sales is called the *all risks yield* (ARY).

Valuation With Different Lease Structures

Lease structures can vary by country. Adjustments must be made when the contract rent (i.e., passing or term rent) and the current market rent (i.e., open market rent) differ. When the lease is renewed, rent is likely to be adjusted to the current market rent.

One way of dealing with the expected change in rent is the *term and reversion approach,* whereby the contract (term) rent and the reversion are appraised separately using different cap rates. The *reversion cap rate* is derived from comparable, fully let, properties. Because the reversion occurs in the future, it must be discounted to the present. The discount rate applied to the contract rent is likely to be lower than the reversion rate because the contract rent is less risky (i.e., the existing tenants are less likely to default on a below-market lease).

A variation of the term and reversion approach is the *layer method.* With the layer method, one source (layer) of income is the contract (term) rent that is assumed to continue in perpetuity. The second layer is the increase in rent that occurs when the lease expires and the rent is reviewed. A cap rate similar to the all risks yield is applied to the term rent because the term rent is less risky. A higher cap rate is applied to the incremental income that occurs as a result of the rent review.

3. The Sales Comparison Approach to Valuation

Under the *sales comparison approach,* the sales prices of similar (comparable) properties are adjusted for differences from the subject property. The differences may relate to size, age, location, property condition, and market conditions at the time of sale. The values of comparable transactions are adjusted upward (downward) for undesirable (desirable) differences with the subject property.

Example: Sales comparison approach

An appraiser has been asked to estimate the value of a warehouse and has collected the following information:

Unit of Comparison	Subject Property	Comparable Transactions		
		1	2	3
Size, in square feet	30,000	40,000	20,000	35,000
Age, in years	5	9	4	5
Physical condition	Average	Good	Average	Poor
Location	Prime	Prime	Secondary	Prime
Sale date, months ago		6	18	12
Sales price		$9,000,000	$4,500,000	$8,000,000

The appraiser's adjustments are based on the following:

- Each adjustment is based on the unadjusted sales price of the comparable.
- Properties depreciate at 2% per annum. Since comparable #1 is 4 years older than the subject, an upward adjustment of $720,000 is made [$9,000,000 × 2% × 4 years].
- Condition adjustment: Good: +5%, average: none; poor: −5%. Since comparable #1 is in better condition than the subject, a downward adjustment of $450,000 is made [$9,000,000 × 5%]. Similarly, an upward adjustment is made for comparable #3 to the tune of $400,000 [$8,000,000 × 5%].
- Location adjustment: Prime: none; secondary: 10%. Since both comparable #1 and the subject are in a prime location, no adjustment is made.
- Over the past 24 months, sales prices have been appreciating 0.5% per month. Since comparable #1 was sold six months ago, an upward adjustment of $270,000 is made [$9,000,000 × 0.5% × 6 months].

Answer:

Once the adjustments are made for all of the comparable transactions, the adjusted sales price per square foot of the comparable transactions are averaged and applied to the subject property as follows:

Adjustments	Subject Property	Comparable Transactions		
		1	2	3
Sales price		$9,000,000	$4,500,000	$8,000,000
Age		+720,000	–90,000	—
Condition		–450,000	—	+400,000
Location		—	+450,000	—
Sale date		+270,000	+405,000	+480,000
Adjusted sales price		$9,540,000	$5,265,000	$8,880,000
Size in square feet	30,000	40,000	20,000	35,000
Adjusted sales price per SF		$238.50	$263.25	$253.71
Average sales price per SF	$251.82			
Estimated value	$7,554,600			

Financial Ratios in Real Estate Lending/Investing

Lenders often use the *debt service coverage ratio* (DSCR) and the *loan-to-value* (LTV) ratio to determine the maximum loan amount on a specific property. The maximum loan amount is based on the measure that results in the lowest debt.

The DSCR is calculated as follows:

$$DSCR = \frac{\text{first year NOI}}{\text{debt services}}$$

The LTV ratio is calculated as follows:

$$LTV = \frac{\text{loan amount}}{\text{appraised value}}$$

When debt is used to finance real estate, equity investors often calculate the *equity dividend rate*, also known as the cash-on-cash return, which measures the cash return on the amount of cash invested.

$$\text{equity dividend rate} = \frac{\text{first year cash flow}}{\text{equity}}$$

The equity dividend rate only covers one period. It is not the same as the IRR that measures the return over the entire holding period.

PUBLICLY TRADED REAL ESTATE SECURITIES
Cross-Reference to CFA Institute Assigned Topic Review #40

Publicly traded real estate securities can take several forms. The main types are real estate investment trusts (REITs), real estate operating companies (REOCs), and residential or commercial mortgage-backed securities (MBS).

Advantages/Disadvantages of Investing in Publicly Traded Real Estate Securities

- Advantages of investing in publicly traded real estate securities include superior liquidity, lower minimum investment, access to premium properties, active professional management, protections afforded to publicly traded securities, and greater diversification potential.
- Advantages of investing in REITs (but not REOCs) include exemption from corporate taxation, predictable earnings, and higher yield.
- Disadvantages of investing in publicly traded real estate securities include lower tax efficiency compared to direct ownership, lack of control, costs of a publicly traded corporate structure, volatility associated with market pricing, limited potential for income growth, forced equity issuance, and structural conflicts of interests.

Due Diligence Considerations of REITs

REIT investors need to pay special attention to:

- Remaining lease terms.
- Inflation protection.
- In-place rents versus market rents.
- Costs to re-lease space.
- Tenant concentration in the portfolio.
- Tenants' financial health.
- New competition.

- Balance sheet analysis.
- Quality of management.

Figure 2: Characteristics of REIT Property Subtypes

	Characteristic			
REIT Type	*Economic Value Determinant*	*Investment Characteristics*	*Principal Risks*	*Due Diligence Considerations*
Shopping/ Retail	1) Retail sales growth 2) Job creation	Stable revenue stream over the short term	Depends on consumer spending	Per-square-foot sales and rental rates
Office	1) Job creation 2) New space supply vs. demand	• Long (5–25 year) lease terms • Stable year-to-year income	Changes in office vacancy and rental rates	• New space under construction • Quality of office space (location, condition of building, etc.)
Residential	1) Population growth 2) Job creation	• One-year leases • Stable	• Competition • Inducements • Regional economy • Inflation of operating costs	• Demographics and income trends • Age and competitive appeal • Cost of home ownership • Rent controls
Health care	1) Population growth 2) New space supply vs. demand	• REITs lease facilities to health care providers • Leases are usually net leases	• Demographics • Government funding • Construction cycles • Financial condition of operators • Tenant litigation	• Operating trends • Government funding trends • Litigation settlements • Insurance costs • Competitors' new facilities vs. demand

Figure 2: Characteristics of REIT Property Subtypes (continued)

	Characteristic			
REIT Type	*Economic Value Determinant*	*Investment Characteristics*	*Principal Risks*	*Due Diligence Considerations*
Industrial	1) Retail sales growth 2) Population growth	• Less cyclical than some other REIT types • 5–25-year net leases • Change in income and values are slow	Shifts in the composition of local and national industrial bases and trade	• Trends in tenants' requirements • Obsolescence of existing space • Need for new types of space • Proximity to transportation • Trends in local supply and demand
Hotel	1) Job creation 2) New space supply vs. demand	• Variable income • Sector is cyclical because it is not protected by long-term leases	• Exposed to business-cycle • Changes in business and leisure travel • Exposure to travel disruptions	• Occupancy, room rates, and operating profit margins vs. industry averages • RevPAR • Trends in forward bookings • Maintenance expenditures • New construction in local markets • Financial leverage
Storage	1) Population growth 2) Job creation	Space is rented under gross leases and on a monthly basis	Ease of entry can lead to overbuilding	• Construction of new competitive facilities • Trends in housing sales • Demographic trends • New business start-up activity • Seasonal trends in demand for storage facilities (can be significant in some markets)

Approaches to REIT Valuation

1. **Net asset value per share:** NAVPS is based on market values and is considered to be the fundamental measure of value for REITs and REOCs.

    NAVPS is the (per share) amount by which assets exceed liabilities, using current market values rather than accounting book values. The current market values for real estate assets are measured by capitalizing NOI (as discussed earlier) or by using a multiple. The market values of other assets and liabilities are assumed to be equal to their book values.

2. **Relative value:** REITs and REOCs can be valued using market-based approaches by applying a multiple to a property's *funds from operations* (FFO) or *adjusted funds from operations* (AFFO).

    Funds from operations: FFO adjusts reported earnings and is a popular measure of the continuing operating income of a REIT or REOC. FFO is calculated as follows:

    > accounting net earnings
    > \+ depreciation charges (expenses)
    > \+ deferred tax charges (i.e., deferred tax expenses)
    > <u>− gains (losses) from sales of property and debt restructuring</u>
    > = funds from operations (FFO)

    Price-to-FFO approach:

    > funds from operations (FFO)
    > <u>÷ shares outstanding</u>
    > = FFO / share
    > <u>× sector average P/FFO multiple</u>
    > = NAV / share

    Adjusted funds from operations: AFFO is an extension of FFO that is intended to be a more useful representation of current economic income.

    > FFO (funds from operations)
    > − non-cash (straight-line) rent adjustment
    > <u>− recurring maintenance-type capital expenditures and leasing commissions</u>
    > = AFFO (adjusted funds from operations)

AFFO is considered a better measure of economic income than FFO because AFFO considers the capital expenditures that are required to sustain the property's economic income. However, FFO is more frequently cited in practice because AFFO relies more on estimates and is considered more subjective.

Price-to-AFFO approach:

> funds from operations (FFO)
> – non-cash rents
> – recurring maintenance-type capital expenditures
> = AFFO
> ÷ shares outstanding
> = AFFO / share
> × property subsector average P/AFFO multiple
> = NAV / share

3. **Discounted cash flow:** Dividend discount models typically include two or three stages, based on near- and long-term growth forecasts. Discounted cash flow models use intermediate-term cash flow projections, plus a terminal value based on historical cash flow multiples.

   value of a REIT share
   = PV(dividends for years 1 through n) + PV(terminal value at the end of year n)

PRIVATE EQUITY
Cross-Reference to CFA Institute Assigned Topic Review #41

Sources of Value Creation

It is commonly believed that PE firms have the ability to add greater value to their portfolio companies than do publicly governed firms. The sources of this increased value are thought to come from the following:

1. The ability to re-engineer the firm and operate it more efficiently.

2. The ability to obtain debt financing on more advantageous terms.

3. Superior alignment of interests between management and private equity ownership.

Control Mechanisms

Private equity firms use a variety of mechanisms to align their interests with those of the managers of portfolio companies. The following contract terms are contained in the term sheet that specifies the terms of the private equity firm's investment.

Compensation: Managers of the portfolio companies receive compensation that is closely linked to the firm's performance.

Tag-along, drag-along clauses: Any time an acquirer acquires control of the company, they must extend the acquisition offer to all shareholders, including firm management.

The term sheet also contains the following provisions that protect the private equity firm by providing it greater control and equity, some of which are triggered by specific events.

Board representation: The private equity firm is ensured control through board representation if the firm experiences a major event such as a takeover, restructuring, initial public offering (IPO), bankruptcy, or liquidation.

Noncompete clauses: Company founders must sign such clauses that prevent them from competing against the firm for a prespecified period of time.

Priority in claims: Private equity firms receive their distributions before other owners, often in the form of preferred dividends. They also have priority on the firm's assets if the portfolio company is liquidated.

Required approvals: Changes of strategic importance (e.g., acquisitions, divestitures, and changes in the business plan) must be approved by the private equity firm.

Earn-outs: These are used predominantly in venture capital investments and tie the acquisition price paid by the private equity firm to the portfolio company's future performance over a specific period.

Appropriate control mechanisms in the investment contract allow private equity firms to make investments in companies of considerable risk.

Valuation Characteristics of Venture Capital vs. Buyout

Figure 3: Valuation Characteristics of Venture Capital and Buyout Investments

Characteristic	*Venture Capital Investments*	*Buyout Investments*
Cash Flows	Low predictability with potentially unrealistic projections	Stable and predictable cash flows
Product Market	New product market with uncertain future	Strong market position, with a possible niche position
Products	Product is based on new technology with uncertain prospects	Established products
Asset Base	Weak	Substantial base that can serve as collateral
Management Team	New team although individual members typically have a strong entrepreneurial record	Strong and experienced
Financial Leverage	Low debt use with a majority of equity financing	High amounts of debt with a large percentage of senior debt and substantial amounts of junior and mezzanine debt
Risk Assessment	Risk is difficult to measure due to new technologies, markets, and firm history	Risk can be measured due to industry and firm maturity
Exit	Exit via IPO or firm sale is difficult to forecast	Exit is predictable
Operations	High cash burn rate required due to firm and product immaturity	Potential exists for reduction in inefficiencies
Working Capital Required	Increasing requirements due to growth	Low requirements
Due Diligence Performed by Private Equity Firms	Private equity firms investigate technological and commercial prospects; investigation of financials is limited due to short history	Private equity firms perform extensive due diligence
Goal Setting	Goals are milestones set in business plan and growth strategy	Goals reference cash flows, strategic plan, and business plan

continued on next page

Figure 3: Valuation Characteristics of Venture Capital and Buyout Investments (continued)

Characteristic	Venture Capital Investments	Buyout Investments
Private Equity Investment Returns	High returns come from a few highly successful investments with writeoffs from less successful investments	Low variability in the success of investments with failures being rare
Capital Market Presence	Generally not active in capital markets	Active in capital markets
Sales Transactions	Most firms are sold as a result of the relationship between venture capital firm and entrepreneurs	Firms are typically sold in an auction-type process
Ability to grow through subsequent funding	Firms are less scalable as subsequent funding is typically smaller	Strong performers can increase subsequent funding amounts
Source of general partner's variable revenue	Carried interest is most common, transaction and monitoring fees are less common	Carried interest, transaction fees, and monitoring fees

Figure 4: Valuation Issues for Buyouts vs. Venture Capital Investments

Valuation Issue	Buyout	Venture Capital
Applicability of DCF Method	Frequently used to estimate value of equity	Less frequently used as cash flows are uncertain
Applicability of Relative Value Approach	Used to check the value from DCF analysis	Difficult to use because there may be no true comparable firms
Use of Debt	High	Low as equity is dominant form of financing
Key Drivers of Equity Return	Earnings growth, increase in multiple upon exit, and reduction in the debt	Pre-money valuation, investment, and subsequent dilution

There are four typical **exit routes** for private equity firms: (1) initial public offerings (IPOs), (2) secondary market sales, (3) management buyouts (MBOs), and (4) liquidations.

The general **private equity risk factors** include liquidity risk, unquoted investments risk, competitive environment risk, agency risk, capital risk, regulatory risk, tax risk, valuation risk, diversification risk and market risk.

The **costs of investing in private equity** are significantly higher than with publicly traded securities and include transaction costs, investment vehicle fund setup costs, administrative costs, audit costs, management and performance costs, dilution costs, and placement fees.

Important **economic terms of a private equity fund** include management, transaction fees, carried interest, ratchet, hurdle rate, target fund size, vintage, and the term of the fund.

The **corporate governance terms** in the prospectus provide the legal arrangements for the control of the fund and include key man clauses, performance disclosure and confidentiality, clawback, distribution waterfall, tag-along, drag-along clauses, removal for cause, no-fault divorce, investment restrictions, and co-investment.

Quantitative Measures

The more popular multiples and those specified by GIPS include the following:

PIC (paid-in capital). The percent of committed or absolute amount of capital utilized by the GP to date.

DPI (distributed to paid-in capital). The cumulative distributions paid to the LPs divided by the cumulative invested capital. It is net of management fees and carried interest and is also referred to as the cash-on-cash return.

RVPI (residual value to paid-in capital). This measures the LP's unrealized return and is the value of the LP's holdings in the fund divided by the cumulative invested capital. It is net of management fees and carried interest.

TVPI (total value to paid-in capital). This measures the LP's realized and unrealized return and is the sum of DPI and RVPI. It is net of management fees and carried interest.

The fraction (f) of the firm that a venture capital investor must own as a result of a new investment (single-round) can be calculated as:

$$\text{NPV method: } f = \frac{\text{new investment}}{\text{present value of entire firm value at exit}}$$

$$\text{IRR method: } f = \frac{\text{future value of new investment at exit}}{\text{future value of entire firm value at exit}}$$

These will be equal as long as the discount factor for the NPV method is equal to the rate of growth used for future value in the IRR method.

A Primer on Commodity Investing
Cross-Reference to CFA Institute Assigned Topic Review #42

Hedgers vs. Speculators

Hedgers may be either producers (i.e., long) or users (i.e., short) of commodities. To hedge their existing exposure, producers (users) will take the short (long) position in the **commodity futures** markets. **Speculators** have no underlying exposure to commodities and demand a premium to provide liquidity (i.e., take the opposite side of a trade).

Convenience Yield

The monetary benefit from holding a physical commodity versus being long the equivalent futures contract is called the convenience yield. Convenience yield reflects the market's expectations about future availability of a resource. Differences between spot prices and futures prices are driven by convenience yield as well as by storage costs. The theory of storage explains that there is an inverse relationship between inventories and commodity futures prices: the higher inventories are, the lower the convenience yield will be.

Ways of Investing in Commodities

- *Physical goods:* Direct exposure but incurs storage costs.
- *Commodity stocks:* Efficiently priced by the market but may have low correlation with the underlying commodity.
- *Commodity mutual funds:* Provide diversification and low transaction costs but funds vary in their management styles and allocation strategy.
- *Commodity futures:* Offer efficiency, low transaction costs, and high leverage, but require rolling of expiring contracts.

- *ETF on a commodity index:* A safe and liquid investment with low transaction costs, though returns are dependent on the index being tracked.
- *Commodity index certificates:* Can be issued quickly and cheaply, but are typically based on excess return and will underperform total return when interest rates are high.

Commodity Term Structure

Backwardation: The situation where the term structure has a negative trend: futures prices are lower than the current spot price. When many hedgers go short in the futures market, the futures price is likely to be less than the *expected future spot price*; this is known as **normal backwardation**.

Contango: The term structure has a positive slope and the futures price is above the spot price.

Commodity Futures Return

total return = spot return + roll return + collateral return + rebalancing return

where:

spot return	= the percentage change in a commodity's spot price
roll return	= the return from closing out maturing futures contracts and replacing them with newer futures contracts. Backwardation will result in a positive roll return, while contango will result in a negative roll return.
collateral return	= return on the posted collateral (which is invested in government securities)
rebalancing return	= additional return on a portfolio of commodity futures contracts when the portfolio is periodically rebalanced. Does not apply to individual contracts.

Commodity Return Theories

Insurance perspective: A long position in commodities will earn positive returns (speculator's premium) in exchange for supporting short hedgers.

Hedging pressure hypothesis: A risk premium can be earned on either long or short positions depending on the balance of hedgers in the market.

Theory of storage: Commodities that are difficult to store will earn a positive convenience yield.

Fixed Income

Topic Weight on Exam	10–20%
SchweserNotes™ Reference	Book 4, Pages 140–276

The Term Structure and Interest Rate Dynamics
Cross-Reference to CFA Institute Assigned Topic Review #43

This topic review discusses the theories and implications of the term structure of interest rates. In addition to understanding the relationships between spot rates, forward rates, yield to maturity, and the shape of the yield curve, be sure you become familiar with concepts like the z-spread, the TED spread, and the LIBOR-OIS spread and key rate duration.

Spot Rates and Forward Rates

The spot rate for a particular maturity is equal to a geometric average of the current one-period spot rate and a series of one-period forward rates.

When the spot curve is flat, forward rates will equal spot rates. When the spot curve is upward sloping (downward sloping), forward rate curves will be above (below) the spot curve, and the yield for a maturity of T will be less than (greater than) the spot rate S_T.

Evolution of Spot Rates in Relation to Forward Rates

If spot rates evolve as predicted by forward rates, bonds of all maturities will realize a one-period return equal to the one-period spot rate, and the forward price will remain unchanged.

Active bond portfolio management is built on the presumption that the current forward curve may not accurately predict future spot rates. Managers attempt to outperform the market by making predictions about how spot rates will evolve relative to the rates suggested by forward rate curves.

If an investor believes that future spot rates will be lower than corresponding forward rates, the investor will purchase bonds (at a presumably attractive price) because the market appears to be discounting future cash flows at "too high" a discount rate.

"Riding the Yield Curve"

When the yield curve is upward sloping, bond managers may use the strategy of "riding the yield curve" to chase above-market returns. By holding long-maturity (relative to their investment horizon) bonds, the manager earns an excess return as the bond "rolls down the yield curve" (i.e., approaches maturity and increases in price). As long as the yield curve remains upward sloping, this strategy will add to the return of a bond portfolio.

The Swap Rate Curve

The swap rate curve provides a benchmark measure of interest rates. It is similar to the yield curve except that the rates used represent the interest rates of the fixed-rate leg in an interest rate swap.

Market participants prefer the swap rate curve as a benchmark interest rate curve rather than a government bond yield curve for the following reasons:

- Swap rates reflect the credit risk of commercial banks rather than governments.
- The swap market is not regulated by any government.
- The swap curve typically has yield quotes at many maturities.

Institutions like wholesale banks are familiar with swaps and, as a result, often use swap curves (rather than other interest rate benchmarks) to value their assets and liabilities.

We define swap spread as the additional interest rate paid by the fixed-rate payer of an interest rate swap over the rate of the "on-the-run" government bond of the same maturity.

swap spread = (swap rate) – (Treasury bond yield)

The Z-spread

The Z-spread is the spread that, when added to each spot rate on the yield curve, makes the present value of a bond's cash flows equal to the bond's market price. The Z refers to zero volatility—a reference to the fact that the Z-spread assumes interest rate volatility is zero. Z-spread is not appropriate to use to value bonds with embedded options.

The TED spread

TED spread = (three-month LIBOR rate) − (three-month T-bill rate)

The TED spread is used as an indication of the overall level of credit risk in the economy.

The LIBOR-OIS Spread

The LIBOR-OIS spread is the amount by which the LIBOR rate (which includes credit risk) exceeds the overnight indexed swap (OIS) rate (which includes only minimal credit risk). The LIBOR-OIS spread is a useful measure of credit risk and provides an indication of the overall well-being of the banking system.

Traditional Theories of the Term Structure of Interest Rates

There are several traditional theories that attempt to explain the term structure of interest rates:

Unbiased expectations theory—Forward rates are an unbiased predictor of future spot rates. Also known as the pure expectations theory.

Local expectations theory—Preserves the risk-neutrality assumption only for short holding periods, while over longer periods, risk premiums should exist. This implies that over short time periods, every bond (even long-maturity risky bonds) should earn the risk-free rate.

Liquidity preference theory—Investors demand a liquidity premium that is positively related to a bond's maturity.

Segmented markets theory—The shape of the yield curve is the result of the interactions of supply and demand for funds in different market (i.e., maturity) segments.

Preferred habitat theory—Similar to the segmented markets theory, but recognizes that market participants will deviate from their preferred maturity habitat if compensated adequately.

Modern Term Structure Models

Two major classes of these modern term structure models are:

1. **Equilibrium term structure models**
   - **Cox-Ingersoll-Ross (CIR) model:**

   $$dr = a(b - r)dt + \sigma\sqrt{r}dz$$

   Assumes the economy has a natural long-run interest rate (b) that the short-term rate (r) converges to.

   - **Vasicek model:**

   $$dr = a(b - r)dt + \sigma dz$$

   Similar to the CIR model but assumes that interest rate volatility level is independent of the level of short-term interest rates.

2. **Arbitrage-free models**—Begins with observed market prices and the assumption that securities are correctly priced.
   - **Ho-Lee model:**

   $$dr_t = \theta_t dt + \sigma dz_t$$

   This model is calibrated by using market prices to find the time-dependant drift term θ_t that generates the *current* term structure.

Managing Bond Exposure to the Factors Driving the Yield Curve

We can measure a bond's exposure to the factors driving the yield curve in a number of ways:

1. **Effective duration**—Measures the sensitivity of a bond's price to parallel shifts in the benchmark yield curve.

2. **Key rate duration**—Measures bond price sensitivity to a change in a specific spot rate, keeping everything else constant.

3. **Sensitivity to parallel, steepness, and curvature movements**—Measures sensitivity to three distinct categories of changes in the shape of the benchmark yield curve.

THE ARBITRAGE-FREE VALUATION FRAMEWORK
Cross-Reference to CFA Institute Assigned Topic Review #44

This topic review introduces valuation of fixed-income securities using spot rates, as well as using the backward induction methodology in a binomial interest rate tree framework.

Valuation of bonds using a zero-coupon yield curve (also known as the spot rate curve) is suitable for option-free bonds. However, for bonds with embedded options where the value of the option varies with outcome of unknown forward rates, a model that allows for variability of forward rates is necessary. One such model is the binomial interest rate tree framework.

Binomial Interest Rate Tree Framework

The binomial interest rate tree framework is a lognormal random walk model with two equally likely outcomes for one-period forward rates at each node. A volatility assumption drives the spread of the nodes in the tree. The tree is calibrated such that (1) the values of benchmark bonds using the tree are equal to the bonds' market prices, (2) adjacent forward rates at any nodal period are two standard deviations apart, and (3) the midpoint for each nodal period is approximately equal to the implied one-period forward rate for that period.

Backward induction is the process of valuing a bond using a binomial interest rate tree. The term *backward* is used because in order to determine the value of a bond at Node 0, we need to know the values that the bond can take on at nodal period 1, and so on.

Example: Valuation of option-free bond using binomial tree

Samuel Favre is interested in valuing a three-year, 3% annual-pay Treasury bond. Favre wants to use a binomial interest rate tree with the following rates:

One-Period Forward Rate in Year

0	1	2
3%	5.7883%	10.7383%
	3.8800%	7.1981%
		4.8250%

Compute the value of the $100 par option-free bond.

Answer:

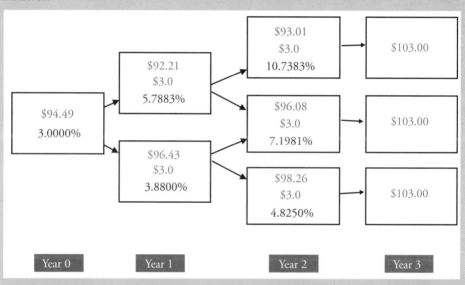

$$V_{2,UU} = \frac{103}{(1.107383)} = \$93.01$$

$$V_{2,UL} = \frac{103}{(1.071981)} = \$96.08$$

$$V_{2,LL} = \frac{103}{(1.048250)} = \$98.26$$

$$V_{1,U} = \frac{1}{2} \times \left[\frac{93.01 + 3}{1.057883} + \frac{96.08 + 3}{1.057883} \right] = \$92.21$$

$$V_{1,L} = \frac{1}{2} \times \left[\frac{96.08 + 3}{1.038800} + \frac{98.26 + 3}{1.038800} \right] = \$96.43$$

$$V_0 = \frac{1}{2} \times \left[\frac{92.21 + 3}{1.03} + \frac{96.43 + 3}{1.03} \right] = \$94.485$$

Pathwise Valuation in a Binomial Interest Rate Framework

In the pathwise valuation approach, the value of the bond is simply the average of the values of the bond at each path. For an n-period binomial tree, there are $2^{(n-1)}$ possible paths.

Monte Carlo Forward-Rate Simulation

The Monte Carlo simulation method uses pathwise valuation and a large number of randomly generated simulated paths. Mortgage-backed securities (MBS) have path-dependent cash flows due to their embedded prepayment option. The Monte Carlo simulation method should be used for valuing MBS as the binomial tree backwards-induction process is inappropriate for securities with path-dependent cash flows.

VALUATION AND ANALYSIS: BONDS WITH EMBEDDED OPTIONS
Cross-Reference to CFA Institute Assigned Topic Review #45

This topic review extends the arbitrage-free valuation framework to valuation of bonds with embedded options. Make sure you understand the risk/return dynamics of embedded options, including their impact on a bond's duration and convexity. Master the concept of OAS and Z-spread. Finally, understand the risk/return characteristics of convertibles.

Callable and Putable Bonds, Straight Bonds, and Embedded Options

Value of an option embedded in a callable or putable bond:

$$V_{call} = V_{straight} - V_{callable}$$

$$V_{put} = V_{putable} - V_{straight}$$

Valuing a Bond with Embedded Options Using Backward Induction

Example: Valuation of call and put options

Consider a two-year, 7% annual-pay, $100 par bond callable in one year at $100. Also consider a two-year, 7% annual-pay, $100 par bond putable in one year at $100.

The interest rate tree at 15% assumed volatility is as given below.

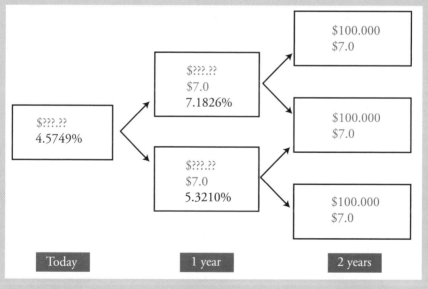

Value the embedded call and put options.

Answer:

Value of the straight (option-free) bond:

Consider the value of the bond at the *upper* node for Period 1, $V_{1,U}$:

$$V_{1,U} = \frac{1}{2} \times \left[\frac{\$100 + \$7}{1.071826} + \frac{\$100 + \$7}{1.071826} \right] = \$99.830$$

Similarly, the value of the bond at the *lower* node for Period 1, $V_{1,L}$, is:

$$V_{1,L} = \frac{1}{2} \times \left[\frac{\$100 + \$7}{1.053210} + \frac{\$100 + \$7}{1.053210} \right] = \$101.594$$

Now calculate V_0, the current value of the bond at Node 0.

$$V_0 = \frac{1}{2} \times \left[\frac{\$99.830 + \$7}{1.045749} + \frac{\$101.594 + \$7}{1.045749} \right] = \$102.999$$

The completed binomial tree is shown below:

Valuing a Two-Year, 7.0% Coupon, Option-Free Bond

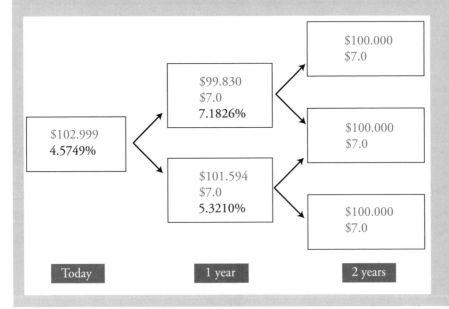

©2016 Kaplan, Inc.

Value of the callable bond:

The call rule (call the bond if the price exceeds $100) is reflected in the boxes in the completed binomial tree, where the second line of the boxes at the one-year node is the lower of the call price or the computed value. For example, the value of the bond in one year at the lower node is $101.594. However, in this case, the bond will be called, and the investor will only receive $100. Therefore, for valuation purposes, the value of the bond in one year at this node is $100.

$$V_{1,L} = \$100$$

$$V_{1,U} = (107 / 1.071826) = \$99.830$$

The calculation for the current value of the bond at Node 0 (today), assuming the simplified call rules of this example, is:

$$V_0 = \frac{1}{2} \times \left[\frac{\$99.830 + \$7}{1.045749} + \frac{\$100.00 + \$7}{1.045749} \right] = \$102.238$$

The completed binomial tree is shown below:

Valuing a Two-Year, 7.0% Coupon, Callable Bond, Callable in One Year at 100

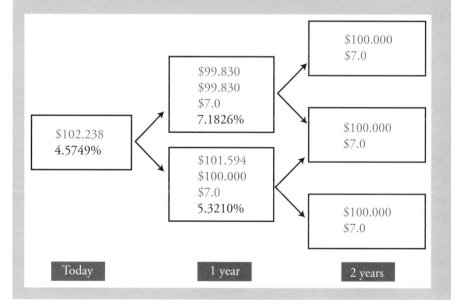

Value of the putable bond:

Similarly, for a putable bond, the put rule is to put the bond if the value falls below $100. The put option would therefore be exercised at the upper-node in year 1 and hence the $99.830 computed value is replaced by the exercise price of $100.

$$V_{1,U} = 100$$

$$V_{1,L} = (107 / 1.053210) = \$101.594$$

$$V_0 = \frac{1}{2} \times \left[\frac{100+7}{1.045749} + \frac{101.594+7}{1.045749} \right] = \$103.081$$

Value of the embedded options:

$$V_{call} = V_{straight} - V_{callable} = \$102.999 - \$102.238 = \$0.76$$

$$V_{put} = V_{putable} - V_{straight} = \$103.081 - \$102.999 = 0.082$$

Impact on Values

When interest rate volatility increases, the value of both call and put options on bonds increase. As volatility increases, the value of a callable bond decreases (remember that the investor is *short* the call option) and the value of a putable bond increases (remember that the investor is *long* the put option).

The short call in a callable bond limits the investor's upside when rates decrease, while the long put in a putable bond hedges the investor against rate increases.

The value of the call option will be lower in an environment with an upward-sloping yield curve because the probability of the option going in the money is low. A call option gains value when the upward-sloping yield curve flattens. Conversely, a put option will have a higher probability of going in the money when the yield curve is upward sloping; the option loses value if the upward-sloping yield curve flattens.

Option-Adjusted Spreads

The option-adjusted spread (OAS) is the constant spread added to each forward rate in a benchmark binomial interest rate tree, such that the sum of the present values of a credit risky bond's cash flows equals its market price. (The actual computation of OAS is an iterative process outside the scope of the curriculum.)

Binomial trees generated under an assumption of high interest rate volatility will lead to higher values for a call option and a corresponding lower value for a callable bond. Under a high volatility assumption, we would already have a lower computed value for the callable bond and, hence, the additional spread (i.e., the OAS) needed to force the discounted value to equal the market price will be lower.

When an analyst uses a lower-than-actual (higher-than-actual) level of volatility, the *computed* OAS for a *callable* bond will be too high (too low) and the callable bond will be erroneously classified as underpriced (overpriced).

Similarly, when the analyst uses a lower-than-actual (higher-than-actual) level of volatility, the *computed* OAS for a *putable* bond will be too low (high) and the putable bond will be erroneously classified as overpriced (underpriced).

Effective Duration

$$\text{effective duration} = \text{ED} = \frac{\text{BV}_{-\Delta y} - \text{BV}_{+\Delta y}}{2 \times \text{BV}_0 \times \Delta y}$$

effective duration (callable/putable) $\le$ effective duration (straight)

effective duration (zero) $\approx$ maturity of the bond

effective duration of floater $\approx$ time in years to next reset

Evaluating the Interest Rate Sensitivity of Bonds with Embedded Options

For bonds with embedded options, one-sided durations—durations when interest rates rise versus when they fall—are better at capturing interest rate sensitivity than regular effective durations. When the underlying option is at- or near-the-money, callable (putable) bonds will have lower (higher) one-sided down-duration than one-sided up-duration.

Callable bonds with low coupon rates are unlikely to be called and, hence, their maturity-matched rate is their most critical rate (and will be the highest key rate duration).

As the coupon rate increases, a callable bond is more likely to be called, and the time-to-exercise rate will start dominating the time-to-maturity rate.

Putable bonds with high coupon rates are unlikely to be put and are most sensitive to its maturity-matched rate. As the coupon rate decreases, a putable bond is more likely to be put and the time-to-exercise rate will start dominating the time-to-maturity rate.

Effective Convexities of Callable, Putable, and Straight Bonds

Straight and putable bonds exhibit positive convexity throughout. Callable bonds also exhibit positive convexity when rates are high. However, at lower rates, callable bonds exhibit negative convexity.

Defining Features of a Convertible Bond

The owner of a convertible bond can exchange the bond for the common shares of the issuer; it includes an embedded call option giving the bondholder the right to buy the common stock of the issuer.

Components of a Convertible Bond's Value

The conversion ratio is the number of common shares for which a convertible bond can be exchanged.

conversion value = market price of stock × conversion ratio

market conversion price = market price of convertible bond / conversion ratio

market conversion premium per share = market conversion price − market price

The minimum value at which a convertible bond trades is its straight value or its conversion value, whichever is greater.

Valuing a Convertible Bond in an Arbitrage-Free Framework

The value of a bond with embedded options can be calculated as the value of the straight bond plus (minus) the value of options that the investor is long (short).

callable and putable convertible bond value = straight value of bond
+ value of call option on stock
− value of call option on bond
+ value of put option on bond

Risk–Return Characteristics of a Convertible Bond

- The major benefit from investing in convertible bonds is the price appreciation resulting from an increase in the value of the common stock.
- The main drawback of investing in a convertible bond versus investing directly in the stock is that when the stock price rises, the bond will underperform the stock because of the conversion premium of the bond.
- If the stock price remains stable, the return on the bond may exceed the stock returns due to the coupon payments received from the bond.
- If the stock price falls, the straight value of the bond limits downside risk (assuming bond yields remain stable).

CREDIT ANALYSIS MODELS
Cross-Reference to CFA Institute Assigned Topic Review #46

Credit Risk Measures

Probability of default is the probability that a borrower (i.e., the bond issuer) fails to pay interest or repay principal when due. **Loss given default** refers to the value a bond investor will lose if the issuer defaults. **Expected loss** is equal to the probability of default multiplied by the loss given default.

The **present value of expected loss** adjusts the expected loss measure by incorporating time value and by using risk-neutral probabilities instead of default probabilities. The present value of expected loss is the difference between the value of a credit-risky bond and an otherwise identical risk-free bond.

Credit Ratings and Credit Scores

Credit ratings and credit scores are ordinal rankings of credit quality. While simple and easy to understand, credit ratings do not adjust with business cycles, and the stability in ratings comes at the expense of a reduction in correlation with default probabilities.

Structural Models of Corporate Credit Risk

Structural models of corporate credit risk are based on the structure of a company's balance sheet and rely on insights provided by option pricing theory. Stock of a company with risky debt outstanding can be viewed as a call option on the company's assets. If the value of the assets exceeds the face value of the debt, the shareholders receive the residual after paying the debt investors. If, on the other hand, the assets are insufficient to cover the face value of the debt, the value of the stock is zero (due to limited liability).

$$\text{value of stock}_T = \max[A_T - K, 0]$$

$$\text{value of debt}_T = \min[K, A_T]$$

where:
A_T = value of company's assets at maturity of debt (at $t = T$)
K = face value of debt

Debt investors can also be thought of as being short a put option on company assets; when the assets are insufficient to cover the face value of debt, shareholders can exercise the put option to sell the assets at face value to pay off the debt.

$$\text{value of risky debt} = \text{value of risk-free debt} - \\ \text{value of a put option on the company's assets}$$

Structural models assume that the company's assets trade in a frictionless market with return of μ and variance of σ^2 (this assumption severely limits the utility of structural models). The risk-free rate is also assumed to be constant and the company's balance sheet is assumed to be simple (i.e., only a single issue of risky debt).

Because historical asset returns are not available, implicit estimation techniques are needed for input parameters of the structural models.

Reduced Form Models of Corporate Credit Risk

Reduced form models do not impose assumptions on the company's balance sheet; instead, they impose assumptions on the output of a structural model. Reduced form models also allow the analyst flexibility to incorporate real world conditions in the model. The inputs for reduced form models can be estimated using historical data; this is called hazard rate estimation. Reduced form models assume that the company has at least one issue of risky zero-coupon debt outstanding. The risk-free rate, probability of default, and recovery rate are all allowed to vary with the state of the economy.

A major strength (and advantage over structural models) is that input estimates are observable and hence historical estimation procedures can be utilized. However, the model should be back-tested properly, otherwise the hazard rate estimation procedures (using past observations to predict the future) may not be valid.

Term Structure of Credit Spreads

Credit spread is the difference between the yield on a zero-coupon *credit-risky* bond and the yield on a zero-coupon *risk-free* bond. The term structure of credit spread captures the relationship between credit spread and maturity.

Present Value of Expected Loss on a Bond

Present value of expected loss is the difference between the value of a risk-free bond and the value of a similar risky bond. This is the maximum amount an investor would pay an insurer to bear the credit risk of a risky bond. We can estimate the present value of expected loss from the credit spread on a risky bond (given the risk-free rate).

Credit Analysis of ABS vs. Credit Analysis of Corporate Debt

Unlike corporate debt, ABS do not default; rather, losses in an ABS's collateral pool are borne by different tranches of the ABS structure based on the distribution waterfall. Hence, credit analysis of ABS entails evaluation of the collateral pool as well as the distribution waterfall. For this reason, the concept of probability of default does not apply to ABS; instead, we use the probability of loss.

Derivatives

Topic Weight on Exam	5–15%
SchweserNotes™ Reference	Book 5, Pages 1–144

Forward Markets and Contracts
Cross-Reference to CFA Institute Assigned Topic Review #47

A clear understanding of the sources and timing of forward contract settlement payments will enable you to be successful on this portion of the exam without depending on pure memorization of these complex formulas.

Pricing vs. Valuation of Forward Contracts

- The *price* of a forward contract is the price specified in the contract at which the long and short sides have agreed to trade the underlying asset when the contract expires.
- The *value* of a forward contract to each side is the amount of money the counterparty would be willing to pay (or receive) to terminate the contract. It's a zero-sum game, so the value of the long position is equal to the negative of the value of the short position.
- The *no-arbitrage* price of the forward contract (with a maturity of T years) is the price at which the value of the long side and the value of the short side are both equal to zero.

$$FP = S_0 \times (1 + R_f)^T$$

The value of the long position in a forward contract at initiation, during the contract life, and at maturity are shown in Figure 1.

©2016 Kaplan, Inc.

Figure 1: Forward Value of Long Position at Initiation, During the Contract Life, and at Expiration

Time	Forward Contract Valuation (Long Position)
At initiation	Zero, because the contract is priced to prevent arbitrage
During the life of the contract	$S_t - \left[\dfrac{FP}{(1+R_f)^{T-t}} \right]$
At expiration	$S_T - FP$

The value of the short position at any point in time is the negative of the long position.

Forward Contract on a Stock

A stock, a stock portfolio, or an equity index may have expected dividend payments over the life of the contract. In order to price such a contract, we must either adjust the spot price for the present value of the expected dividends (PVD) or adjust the forward price for the future value of the dividends (FVD):

$$FP(\text{on a stock}) = (S_0 - PVD) \times (1 + R_f)^T = \left[S_0 \times (1 + R_f)^T \right] - FVD$$

To calculate the *value* of the long position in a forward contract on a dividend-paying stock, we make the adjustment for the present value of the remaining expected discrete dividends at time t (PVD_t) to get:

$$V_t(\text{long position on a stock}) = (S_t - PVD_t) - \left(\frac{FP}{(1+R_f)^{T-t}} \right)$$

Forward Contract on Equity Index

The dividends on an equity index are approximately continuous, so to price and value a forward contract on an equity index, use the same basic formulas with continuous compounding at the continuously compounded risk-free rate of R_f^c and assume a continuous dividend yield of δ^c.

$$FP(\text{on equity index}) = S_0 \times e^{\left(R_f^c - \delta^c \right) \times T}$$

$$V_t(\text{long position on equity index}) = \left(\frac{S_t}{e^{\delta^c \times (T-t)}} \right) - \left(\frac{FP}{e^{R_f^c \times (T-t)}} \right)$$

Forwards on Fixed Income Securities

To calculate the no-arbitrage forward price and value on a coupon-paying bond, substitute the present value of the expected coupon payments (PVC) *over the life of the contract* for the present value of the expected dividends to get:

$$FP(\text{on fixed income security}) = (S_0 - PVC) \times (1 + R_f)^T$$

$$V_t(\text{long position on fixed income security}) = (S_t - PVC_t) - \left(\frac{FP}{(1 + R_f)^{T-t}}\right)$$

Forward Rate Agreements (FRAs)

Basics of FRAs:

- The long position in an FRA is the party that would borrow the money (long the loan with the contract price being the interest rate on the loan).
- If LIBOR at expiration is above the rate specified in the forward agreement, the long position in the contract can be viewed as the right to borrow at below market rates, and the long will receive a payment.
- If rates at the expiration date are below the then-current market rates, the short will receive a cash payment from the long. (The right to lend at *above* market rates would have a positive value.)
- The notation for FRAs is unique. For example, a 2×3 FRA is a contract that expires in two months (60 days), and the underlying loan is settled in three months (90 days). The underlying rate is 1-month (30-day) LIBOR on a 30-day loan in 60 days. A timeline for a 2×3 FRA is shown in Figure 2.

Figure 2: Illustration of a 2×3 FRA

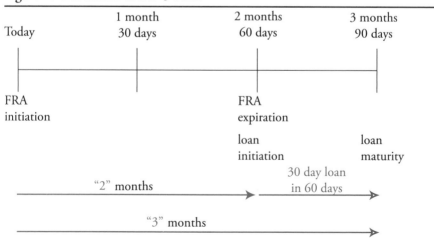

©2016 Kaplan, Inc.

Pricing an FRA

The "price" of the FRA is actually the forward interest rate implied by the spot rates consistent with the FRA. For example, the "price" of the 2×3 FRA is the 30-day forward rate in 60 days implied by the 60- and 90-day spot rates.

Valuing an FRA

The value of an FRA to the long or short position comes from the interest savings on a loan to be made at the settlement date. This value is to be received at the end of the loan, so the value of an FRA after initiation is the present value of these savings. Remember, if the rate in the future is less than the FRA rate, the long is "obligated to borrow" at above-market rates and will have to make a payment to the short. If the rate is greater than the FRA rate, the long will receive a payment from the short.

Let's outline the general steps for valuing a 2×3 FRA (a 30-day loan in 60 days) 40 days after initiation (which means there are 20 days remaining until the FRA expires).

Step 1: Calculate the implied *30-day forward rate* at the settlement date, 20 days from now, using the current 20-day spot rate and the current 50-day spot rate.

Step 2: Calculate the value of the FRA at maturity as the notional principal times the difference between the forward rate from Step 1 and the original FRA "price." Make sure to convert from an annual rate to a 30-day rate. If the current forward rate is greater than the original FRA price, the long position has positive value. If the current forward rate is less than the original FRA price, the short position has positive value.

Step 3: Calculate the value of the FRA today by discounting the value at maturity from Step 2 at the 50-day spot rate.

Currency Forwards

The pricing and valuation of a currency forward contract is straightforward. The calculation of the currency forward rate is an application of covered interest parity from the topic review of international parity relations in Study Session 4.

Covered interest rate parity gives us the no-arbitrage forward price of a unit of foreign currency in terms of the home currency (DC/FC) for a currency forward contract:

$$F_T = \left(\text{currency forward contract}\right) = S_0 \times e^{\left(R^c_{DC} - R^c_{FC}\right) \times T}$$

F and *S* are quoted in domestic currency units per one unit of foreign currency.

At any time prior to maturity, the value of a currency forward contract to the long will depend on the spot rate at time t and S_t:

$$V_t(\text{currency forward contract}) = \left[\frac{S_t}{\left(1+R_{FC}\right)^{T-t}}\right] - \left[\frac{F_t}{\left(1+R_{DC}\right)^{T-t}}\right]$$

FUTURES MARKETS AND CONTRACTS
Cross-Reference to CFA Institute Assigned Topic Review #48

Pricing Futures Contracts

The no-arbitrage price of a futures contract on an asset with no storage costs or cash flows is approximately the same as that of a forward contract on the asset:

$$FP = S_0 \times (1 + R_f)^T$$

However, the mark-to-market feature of futures contracts will cause futures and forward prices to be slightly different.

Figure 3: Prices of Futures vs. Forward Contracts

If the correlation between the underlying asset value and interest rates is…	Investors will…
Positive	Prefer to go long in a **futures contract** and the futures price will be greater than the price of an otherwise comparable forward contract
Zero	Have no preference
Negative	Prefer to go long in a **forward contract** and the forward price will be greater than the price of an otherwise comparable futures contract

Valuing Futures Contracts

Futures contracts are marked-to-market daily, so the value to both sides of the contract is zero at the end of the trading day. Therefore, the contract only has value during the trading day:

futures contract value = current futures price − futures price at last mark-to-market

©2016 Kaplan, Inc.

Futures Arbitrage

If the futures contract is overpriced (actual futures market price is greater than the no-arbitrage price), *cash-and-carry arbitrage* will generate a riskless profit:

- At the initiation of the contract:
  1. Borrow money for the term of the contract at the risk-free rate.
  2. Buy the underlying asset at the spot price.
  3. Sell a futures contract at the current futures price.

- At contract expiration:
  4. Deliver the asset and receive the futures contract price.
  5. Repay the loan plus interest.

If the futures contract is underpriced (futures market price is less than the no-arbitrage price), *reverse cash-and-carry arbitrage* will earn an arbitrage profit:

- At the initiation of the contract:
  1. Sell the asset short.
  2. Lend the short sale proceeds at the risk-free rate.
  3. Buy the futures contract at market price.

- At contract expiration:
  4. Collect loan proceeds.
  5. Take delivery of the asset for the futures price and cover the short sale commitment.

Monetary and Non-Monetary Benefits and Costs of Holding the Underlying Asset

Future prices are affected by the monetary costs and benefits (i.e., net costs, or NC) of holding the underlying asset. Storage and insurance are costs, while any cash flows from the asset are a benefit:

$$FP = S_0 \times (1 + R_f)^T + FV(NC)$$

There can also be *non-monetary benefits* (i.e., net benefits, or NB) from holding assets and having the use of them. This non-monetary return is termed a convenience yield. In that case, the no-arbitrage futures price is:

$$FP = S_0 \times (1 + R_f)^T - FV(NB)$$

Futures Prices as Predictors of Future Asset Prices

One issue in futures pricing is whether the futures price is equal to the expected future price of the asset. Any difference is due to risk (i.e., the uncertainty about the future asset price). If futures buyers are taking risk from asset owners and require a premium for doing so, the futures price will be less than the expected spot price, a situation described as *normal backwardation*.

It is also possible that futures buyers are seeking to reduce the asset price risk they currently have because of their need to purchase the asset in the future. In this case, there may be no risk premium, or even a negative premium, if futures buyers are willing to pay a higher price because of the risk reduction benefits to them of a long futures position. If this results in futures prices greater than expected future spot prices, the situation is referred to as *normal contango*. Note that normal backwardation and normal contango are different from backwardation and contango.

- **Backwardation.** Futures price is less than spot price.
- **Contango.** Futures price is greater than spot price.
- **Normal backwardation.** Futures price is less than *expected* spot price.
- **Normal contango.** Futures price is greater than *expected* spot price.

Eurodollar Contract Pricing Difficulty

Eurodollar futures are priced as a discount yield, and LIBOR-based deposits are priced as an add-on yield. The result is that the deposit value is not perfectly hedged by the Eurodollar contract, so Eurodollar futures can't be priced using the standard no-arbitrage framework.

Pricing Treasury Bond, Equity Index, and Currency Futures

The price of a Treasury **bond future** that settles at time = T is calculated as the future value of the bond minus the future value of the bonds cash flows over the life of the futures contract, adjusted by the conversion factor (CF) of the cheapest-to-deliver (CTD) bond under the terms of the futures contract.

$$FP(\text{T-bond}) = \frac{\text{PV of CTD bond } [(1 + R_f(T)]^T - FV_T \text{ (interest cash flows 0,T)}}{CF(\text{CTD bond})}$$

In order to price equity or *stock index future* of period T, we need to adjust for the dividend yield, either as a discrete annual rate (δ) or a continuously compounded rate (δ^C) to get:

$$FP(\text{Index}) = \frac{S_0}{(1+\delta)^T}(1+R)^T \text{ or in continuous time,}$$

$$FP(\text{Index}) = S_0 e^{(R^C - \delta^C)T}$$

In order to price a currency future, we must take account of the difference in yield between the futures contract currency return (R) and the underlying asset currency return (R_{foreign}):

$$FP(\text{Index}) = \frac{S_0}{(1+R_{\text{foreign}})^T}(1+R)^T \text{ or in continuous time,}$$

$$FP(\text{Index}) = S_0 e^{(R^C - R^C_{\text{foreign}})T}$$

OPTION MARKETS AND CONTRACTS
Cross-Reference to CFA Institute Assigned Topic Review #49

Put-Call Parity for European Options

Put-call parity must hold by arbitrage:

$$C_0 + \left[\frac{X}{(1+R_f)^T}\right] = P_0 + S_0$$

or

call + riskless discount bond = put + stock

or

fiduciary call = protective put

Use put-call parity to create *synthetic instruments*. Interpret "+" as a long position and "–" as a short position:

synthetic call = put + stock – riskless discount bond
synthetic put = call – stock + riskless discount bond
synthetic stock = call – put + riskless discount bond
synthetic riskless discount bond = put + stock – call

Violations of put-call parity are exploited by buying the underpriced component and shorting the overpriced component:

- If fiduciary call > protective put, sell fiduciary call, buy protective put.
- If fiduciary call < protective put, buy fiduciary call, sell protective put.

The Binomial Option Pricing Model (OPM)

The binomial process generates stock price paths, just as the binomial interest rate model generates interest rate paths. However, whereas the probabilities of an up or down movement are the same (equal 0.5) in an interest rate tree, these so-called pseudo probabilities are usually not equal (but still must sum to 1.0) in a stock price tree.

We can calculate the value of an option on the stock by:

- Calculating the payoff of the option at maturity in both the up-move and down-move states.
- Calculating the expected value of the option in one year as the probability-weighted average of the payoffs in each state.
- Discounting the expected value back to today at the risk-free rate.

Let's calculate the *value* today of a 1-period call option on a stock with an exercise price of $30. Suppose the risk-free rate is 7%, the current value of the stock is $30, and the size of an up-move (U) is 1.333, as shown in Figure 4.

Figure 4: 1-Period Binomial Tree

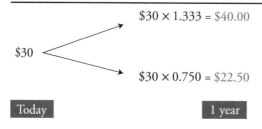

$30 × 1.333 = $40.00

$30

$30 × 0.750 = $22.50

Today   1 year

The size of the downward movement (D) factor is:

$$D = \frac{1}{U} = \frac{1}{1.333} = 0.75$$

The risk-neutral probability of an upward movement is:

$$\pi_U = \frac{1 + R_f - D}{U - D} = \frac{1.07 - 0.75}{1.333 - 0.75} = 0.55$$

The risk-neutral probability of a downward movement is then:

$$\pi_D = 1 - \pi_U = 1 - 0.55 = 0.45$$

The binomial tree for the stock and the option is shown in Figure 5.

Figure 5: 1-Period Call Option With X = $30

$S_0 = \$30$

$\pi_U = 0.55$

$S_1^+ = \$30 \times 1.333 = \$40.00$

$C_1^+ = \max (0, \$40 - \$30) = \$10.00$

$\pi_D = 0.45$

$S_1^- = \$30 \times 0.750 = \$22.50$

$C_1^- = \max (0, \$22.50 - \$30) = \$0$

Today   1 year

The call option is in-the-money in the "up" state, so its terminal value is $10. It is out-of-the-money in the "down" state, so its terminal value is zero.

The expected value of the option in one year is:

$$(\$10 \times 0.55) + (\$0 \times 0.45) = \$5.50$$

The present value of the call option's expected value today is:

$$c = \frac{\$5.50}{1.07} = \$5.14$$

Options on Fixed Income Securities

To price options on bonds, we need a binomial interest rate tree that shows possible future 1-period interest rates. The risk-free rate is not constant, however. Since the tree gives us a series of 1-period rates, we need to discount the payments by one or more of these rates, depending on how many periods the payoff is out (to the right) on the tree.

There are three basic steps to valuing an option on a fixed-income instrument using a binomial tree:

Step 1: Price the bond at each node using the projected interest rates.

Step 2: Establish the intrinsic value of the option at each node at the maturity of the option.

Step 3: Bring the terminal option values determined in Step 2 back to today.

We assume that the probability of an up- and down-move in the interest rate tree is always 50%.

Options on Interest Rates: Caps and Floors

Steps in *valuing a 2-year cap or floor:*

Step 1: Calculate the expiration value of the 2-year caplet or floorlet at each node at the end of year 2 using the appropriate formula:

$$\text{expiration value of caplet} = \frac{\max\left[0, (1\text{-yr. rate} - \text{cap rate}) \times \text{notional prin.}\right]}{1 + 1\text{-yr. rate}}$$

$$\text{expiration value of floorlet} = \frac{\max\left[0, (\text{floor rate} - 1\text{-yr. rate}) \times \text{notional prin.}\right]}{1 + 1\text{-yr. rate}}$$

Step 2: Bring the terminal caplet or floorlet values from Step 1 back to today. The probabilities of up- and down-moves are 50%.

Step 3: Repeat Steps 1 and 2 for the 1-year caplet or floorlet.

Step 4: Calculate the value of the interest rate cap as the sum of values of individual caplets, or the value of the interest rate floor as the sum of values of individual floorlets.

The Black-Scholes-Merton Option Pricing Model Assumptions and Limitations

The *assumptions* underlying the Black-Scholes-Merton (BSM) model are:

- The price of the underlying asset follows a lognormal distribution.
- The (continuous) risk-free rate is constant and known.
- The volatility of the underlying asset is constant and known.
- Markets are frictionless.
- The underlying asset generates no cash flows.
- The options are European.

Because of the limitations of these assumptions, the BSM model is *not appropriate*:

- For valuing interest rate options and options on bond prices because the assumption of a constant and known risk-free rate is violated.
- When the assumption of a constant and known volatility of underlying asset returns is violated.

- In cases where taxes and transactions costs are significant.
- For pricing American-style options.

Inputs to the Black-Scholes-Merton Model

There are five inputs to the BSM model: asset price, exercise price, asset price volatility, time to expiration, and the risk-free rate. The effects of changes in each input (in isolation, holding all else constant) on the value of European call and put options (on assets with no cash flows) are outlined in Figure 6.

Figure 6: BSM Sensitivities

Sensitivity Factor ("Greek")	Input	Calls	Puts
Delta	Asset price (S)	Positively related delta > 0	Negatively related delta < 0
Vega	Volatility (σ)	Positively related vega > 0	Positively related vega > 0
Rho	Risk-free rate (r)	Positively related rho > 0	Negatively related rho < 0
Theta	Time to expiration (T)	Value → $0 as call → maturity theta < 0	Value usually → 0 as put → maturity theta < 0*
	Exercise price (X)	Negatively related	Positively related

* There is an exception to the general rule that European put option thetas are negative. The put value may increase as the option approaches maturity if the option is deep in the money and close to maturity.

Delta

An option's *delta* estimates the change in the value of the option for a 1-unit change in the value of the underlying stock.

$$\text{delta}_{call} = \frac{\text{change in call price}}{\text{change in stock price}}$$

For small changes in stock price, a call option's delta is $N(d_1)$ from the BSM; the comparable put option's delta is $N(d_1) - 1$. The following relationships are approximations:

$$\text{change in call price} \approx N(d_1) \times \text{change in stock price}$$

$$\text{change in put price} \approx [N(d_1) - 1] \times \text{change in stock price}$$

Figure 7: Delta: Key Points to Remember

Option	Range	Far Out-of-the-Money	Far In-the-Money	As Stock Price Increases
Call	0 to 1	Close to 0	Close to 1	Increases from 0 to 1
Put	–1 to 0	Close to 0	Close to –1	Increases from –1 to 0

Delta-Neutral Hedging

A *delta-neutral portfolio* is a combination of short call options with the underlying stock so that the value of the portfolio doesn't change when the value of the stock changes. The number of call options to sell to create the delta-neutral hedge is as follows:

$$\text{number of call options needed to delta hedge} = \frac{\text{number of shares hedged}}{\text{delta of call option}}$$

The delta-neutral position only holds for very small changes in the value of the underlying stock. Hence, the delta-neutral portfolio must be continuously rebalanced to maintain the hedge. This is called a dynamic hedge.

Gamma

Gamma measures the rate of change in delta as the underlying stock price changes. Gamma is largest when the option is at-the-money, so delta is very sensitive to changes in the underlying stock price when the option is at-the-money.

Gamma can be viewed as a measure of how poorly a dynamic hedge will perform when it is not rebalanced in response to a change in the asset price. Hedges with at-the-money options will have higher gammas, and consequently small changes in stock price will lead to large changes in delta and frequent rebalancing.

Options on Forwards and Futures

Put-call parity for options on forwards and futures is:

$$C_0 + \frac{X - F_T}{(1 + R_f)^T} = P_0$$

The Black model can be used to price European options on forwards and futures. The price of a European option on a forward or futures contract is equal to an option on the underlying asset if the options and the forward/futures contract expire at the same time.

Swap Markets and Contracts

Cross-Reference to CFA Institute Assigned Topic Review #50

Pricing vs. Valuation of Swaps

The distinction between pricing and valuing swaps is the same as it is for forward contracts:

- The price of a plain-vanilla swap, for example, is the fixed rate (the swap rate) that makes the present value of the fixed-rate payments equal to the present value of the floating-rate payments. Assuming the fixed rate is set to this rate, the value of the swap to both parties at initiation of the swap is zero.
- After initiation, interest rates change and the present value of the payments on both sides of the plain vanilla swap change. The value of the swap to either party after initiation is the present value of the payments that party will receive less the present value of the payments it will make. Because the swap is a derivative instrument, the total value to both sides must be zero, which means this is a zero-sum game, and the value of one side is the negative of the value of the other side.

Swaps as Combinations of Other Instruments

There is a simple bond transaction that is equivalent to a plain vanilla *interest rate swap*. The fixed payer could gain identical exposure by issuing a fixed-coupon bond and investing the proceeds in a floating rate bond with the same maturity and payment dates. On each payment date, a fixed coupon payment is paid, and the floating rate payment is received.

An *equity swap*, from the perspective of the fixed payer, is equivalent to borrowing at a fixed rate and investing in a stock, a portfolio, or an index. The equivalence is not exact, but close enough as an explanation of the capital markets transactions to approximate the exposure of an equity/fixed swap.

The exposure of a *currency swap* is equivalent to that of issuing a bond in one currency, exchanging the proceeds for another currency at the spot exchange rate, and purchasing a bond denominated in the other currency with the same payment and maturity dates.

Pricing and Valuing a Plain Vanilla Interest Rate Swap

We can price a plain vanilla (fixed-for-floating) interest rate swap by using the insight that the swap is equivalent to issuing a fixed-rate bond and buying an otherwise identical floating rate note. The fixed rate (the swap rate) must be set so that the values of the "replicating" floating-rate bond and the "replicating" fixed-rate bond are the same at swap initiation.

The fixed periodic rate on an N-period swap at initiation (as a percentage of the principal value) can be calculated as:

$$C_N = \left(\frac{1 - Z_N}{Z_1 + Z_2 + \ldots + Z_N} \right)$$

where:
Z_N = present value of $1 to be received on the nth payment date, of N dates

At any payment date, the market value of a swap (to the fixed-rate payer) is the difference between the value of the replicating floating-rate bond and the value of the replicating fixed-rate bond. Since the fixed payer is essentially long a floating-rate bond and short a fixed-rate bond, his position will have positive value only when the fixed-rate bond is trading at a discount to par. This follows from the fact that the floating-rate bond will be valued at par at each payment date.

Between payment dates, we can value the swap by noting that the floating rate at the next payment date will trade at par, so its value prior to the payment date is the present value of the par amount plus the known coupon payment. Commit the following relationships to memory:

value of plain vanilla interest rate swap to *fixed-rate-payer side*

= PV of replicating floating-rate bond – PV of replicating fixed-rate bond

value of plain vanilla interest rate swap to *floating-rate-payer side*

= PV of replicating fixed-rate bond – PV of replicating floating-rate bond

Keep in mind that what we are doing is valuing the interest rate swap by valuing an equivalent position in a fixed-rate bond and floating-rate bond. We calculate the value of the fixed-rate bond as the present value of the expected fixed-rate interest payments and principal payments. We calculate the value of the floating-rate bond the same way. The difference between these two values is the value of the swap. The actual swap, however, doesn't require principal payments, and interest payments are netted.

Pricing and Valuing a Currency Swap

Pricing a currency swap (i.e., determining the swap fixed rate in a currency swap) is accomplished using the same procedure as for interest rate swaps, except that now we have to deal with two term structures (one in each currency) and two swap rates.

©2016 Kaplan, Inc.

For example, in a fixed-for-fixed currency swap where one side pays U.S. dollars fixed and the other side pays Euros fixed, the U.S. dollar fixed rate is determined using the term structure of U.S. dollar rates, and the Euro fixed rate is determined from the term structure of Euro rates.

Valuing a currency swap is also similar to valuing an interest rate swap; we value the "replicating bonds" for each side of the swap, and then the value to each party is calculated as the value of the payments it receives less the value of the payments it makes. However, there is the complicating factor of dealing with two different currencies and an exchange rate between the two currencies that changes over time.

Let's use the fixed-for-fixed U.S. dollar-Euro swap as an example to illustrate the procedure, assuming we are valuing the swap in U.S. dollars.

- Given the notional principal of the swap in dollars, convert to Euros using the exchange rate at the initiation of the swap. The notional principal in dollars is the face value of the replicating U.S. dollar denominated bond; the notional principal in Euros is the face value of the replicating Euro denominated bond.
- After the initiation of the swap, value the U.S. dollar-denominated bond in U.S. dollars and the Euro-denominated bond in Euros using the usual procedure.
- Convert the value of the Euro denominated bond into U.S. dollars using the exchange rate in effect on the date the swap is being valued (which will most likely be different than the original rate used to calculate the notional principals).
- Calculate the value of the swap to each party as the difference between the U.S. dollar values of the two bonds. For example, the value of the swap to the party paying U.S. dollars is the value of the Euro-denominated bond (in U.S. dollars) minus the value of the U.S. dollar-denominated bond (in U.S. dollars).

Equity Swaps

The fixed-rate side of an equity swap is priced and valued just like an interest rate swap. The equity side can be valued by multiplying the notional amount of the contract times one plus the percentage equity appreciation since the last payment date. Use the difference in values to value the swap.

Credit Risk

Credit risk arises because of the possibility that the other party to a swap cannot or will not make the payments required by the swap contract. Several key points to remember include:

- Current credit risk is the credit risk associated with the payment currently due.
- Potential credit risk reflects the future credit risk remaining over the life of the swap.
- For an interest rate swap, potential credit risk is greatest in the middle of the swap term when the credit worthiness of the counter party may have deteriorated since swap initiation, and there are significant payments yet to be made over the remaining term of the swap.
- For a currency swap, the maximum potential credit risk occurs after the middle of the swap term because of the remaining principal payment due at maturity.
- Credit risk can be reduced by:
  - Netting.
  - Marking to market.

Swaptions

A *payer swaption* is the right to enter into a specific swap at some date in the future as the fixed rate payer at a rate specified in the swaption. If swap fixed rates increase (as interest rates increase), the right to enter the pay-fixed side of a swap (a payer swaption) becomes more valuable.

The value of a payer swaption at expiration (if it is in-the-money) is the present value of the difference between swap fixed-rate payments based on the higher existing swap rate and payments based on the strike rate.

A *receiver swaption* is the right to enter into a specific swap at some date in the future as the floating-rate payer at a rate specified in the swaption. A receiver swaption becomes more valuable if rates decrease.

The value of a receiver swaption at expiration (if it is in-the-money) is the present value of the difference in swap fixed-rate payments based on the higher strike rate and the lower existing swap rate.

Uses of Swaptions

A swaption can be used to:

- Hedge an anticipated exposure to fixed or floating interest rate payments.

- Speculate on the direction of interest rates.
- Provide a method of exiting an existing swap prior to the normal termination date.

The *swap spread* is the spread between the swap rate and the comparable maturity T-notes. The swap spread will respond to the same factors as other "quality" spreads.

INTEREST RATE DERIVATIVE INSTRUMENTS
Cross-Reference to CFA Institute Assigned Topic Review #51

Caps, Floors, and Collars

- An *interest rate cap* is an agreement in which one party agrees to pay the other at regular intervals over a certain period of time when the benchmark interest rate (e.g., LIBOR) exceeds the strike rate specified in the contract. This strike rate is called the cap rate. Because an interest rate cap is a multi-period agreement, a cap is actually a portfolio of call options on LIBOR, called caplets. A long cap is also equivalent to a portfolio of long put options on fixed-income security prices.
- An *interest rate floor* is an agreement in which one party agrees to pay the other at regular intervals over a certain time period when the benchmark interest rate (e.g., LIBOR) falls below the strike rate specified in the contract. This strike rate is called the floor rate. Because a floor is a multi-period agreement, a floor is actually a portfolio of put options on LIBOR, called floorlets. A long floor is also equivalent to a portfolio of long call options on fixed-income security prices.
- An *interest rate collar* is a simultaneous position in a floor and a cap on the same benchmark rate over the same period with the same settlement dates. There are two types of collars. The first type of collar is to purchase a cap and sell a floor to hedge a floating rate liability. The second type of collar is to purchase a floor and sell a cap to hedge a floating rate asset.

CREDIT DEFAULT SWAPS
Cross-Reference to CFA Institute Assigned Topic Review #52

Credit Default Swaps

A **credit default swap** (CDS) is a contract between two parties in which one party purchases protection from the other party against losses from the default of a borrower. If a credit event occurs, the *credit protection buyer* gets compensated by the *credit protection seller*. To obtain this coverage, the protection buyer pays the seller a premium called the *CDS spread*. The protection seller is assuming (i.e., long) credit risk, while the protection buyer is short credit risk.

The payoff on a single-name CDS is based on the market value of the *cheapest-to-deliver* (CTD) bond that has the same seniority as the reference obligation. Upon default, a single-name CDS is terminated.

An **index CDS** covers an equally weighted combination of borrowers. When one of the index constituents defaults, there is a payoff and the notional principal is adjusted downward.

CDS Pricing

The factors that influence the pricing (i.e., spread) of CDS include the probability of default, the loss given default, and the coupon rate on the swap. The conditional probability of default (i.e., the probability of default given that default has not already occurred) is called the hazard rate.

$$\text{expected loss}_t = (\text{hazard rate})_t \times (\text{loss given default})_t$$

If the coupon payment on the swap is not set to be equal to the credit spread of the reference obligation, an upfront payment from one of the counterparties to the other is necessary.

$$\text{upfront payment (by protection buyer)} = \text{PV(protection leg)} - \text{PV(premium leg)}$$

or

$$\text{upfront premium} \approx (\text{CDS spread} - \text{CDS coupon}) \times \text{CDS duration}$$

After inception of the swap, the value of the CDS changes as the spread changes.

$$\text{profit for protection buyer (\%)} \approx \text{change in spread (\%)} \times \text{CDS duration}$$

CDS Uses

In a naked CDS, an investor with no exposure to the underlying purchases protection in the CDS market. In a long/short trade, an investor purchases protection on one reference entity while selling protection on another reference entity.

©2016 Kaplan, Inc.

A curve trade is a type of long/short trade where the investor is buying and selling protection on the same reference entity but with different maturities. An investor who believes the short-term outlook for the reference entity is better than the long-term outlook can use a curve-steepening trade (buying protection in a long-term CDS and selling protection in a short-term CDS) to profit if the credit curve steepens. Conversely, an investor who is bearish about the reference entity's prospects in the short term will enter into a curve-flattening trade.

Portfolio Management

Topic Weight on Exam	5–10%
SchweserNotes™ Reference	Book 5, Pages 145–216

An Introduction to Multifactor Models

Cross-Reference to CFA Institute Assigned Topic Review #53

Arbitrage Pricing Theory (APT):

The APT describes the equilibrium relationship between expected returns for well-diversified portfolios and their multiple sources of systematic risk.

Underlying Assumptions of the APT

The APT makes only three key assumptions:

1. Unsystematic risk can be diversified away in a portfolio.

2. Returns are generated using a factor model.

3. No arbitrage opportunities exist.

Arbitrage Opportunities

An arbitrage opportunity is defined as an investment opportunity that bears no risk and has no cost, but provides a profit. Arbitrage is conducted by forming long and short portfolios; the proceeds of the short sale are used to purchase the long portfolio.

Additionally, the factor sensitivities (betas) of the long and short portfolios are identical and, hence, our net exposure to systematic risk is zero. The difference in returns on the long and short portfolios is the arbitrage return.

Expected Return Versus Factor Sensitivities and Factor Risk Premiums

$$\text{expected return} = \text{risk-free rate} + \sum(\text{factor sensitivity}) \times (\text{factor risk premium})$$

Macroeconomic Factor Models, Fundamental Factor Models, and Statistical Factor Models

A multifactor model is an extension of the one-factor market model; in a multifactor model, asset returns are a function of more than one factor. There are three types of multifactor models:

1. Macroeconomic factor models assume that asset returns are explained by surprises (or shocks) in macroeconomic risk factors (e.g., GDP, interest rates, and inflation). Factor surprises are defined as the difference between the realized value of the factor and its consensus expected value.

2. Fundamental factor models assume asset returns are explained by the returns from multiple firm-specific factors (e.g., P/E ratio, market cap, leverage ratio, and earnings growth rate).

3. Statistical factor models use multivariate statistics (factor analysis or principal components) to identify statistical factors that explain the covariation among asset returns. The major weakness is that the statistical factors may not lend themselves well to economic interpretation.

Sources of Active Risk

Active return is the difference between portfolio and benchmark returns ($R_P - R_B$), and active risk is the standard deviation of active return over time. Active risk is determined by the manager's active factor tilt and active asset selection decisions:

active risk squared = active factor risk + active specific risk

Tracking Risk and the Information Ratio

The information ratio is active return divided by active risk:

$$IR = \frac{\overline{R}_P - \overline{R}_B}{s(R_P - R_B)}$$

Multifactor Models' Uses and Output

Multifactor models can be useful for risk and return attribution and for portfolio composition. In return attribution, the difference between an active portfolio's return and the benchmark return is allocated between factor return and security selection return.

$$\text{factor return} = \sum_{i=1}^{k} (\beta_{pk} - \beta_{bk}) \times (\lambda^k)$$

In risk attribution, the sum of the active factor risk and active specific risk is equal to active risk squared (which is the variance of active returns):

active risk squared = active factor risk + active specific risk

$$\text{active specific risk} = \sum_{i=1}^{n} (W_{pi} - W_{bi})^2 \sigma_{\varepsilon i}^2$$

active factor risk = active risk squared − active specific risk

Multifactor models can also be useful for portfolio construction. Passive managers can invest in a tracking portfolio, while active managers can go long or short factor portfolios.

A factor portfolio is a portfolio with a factor sensitivity of 1 to a particular factor and 0 to all other factors. It represents a pure bet on a single factor and can be used for speculation or hedging purposes. A tracking portfolio is a portfolio with a specific set of factor sensitivities. Tracking portfolios are often designed to replicate the factor exposures of a benchmark index like the S&P 500.

Potential Benefits for Investors in Considering Multiple Risk Dimensions When Modeling Asset Returns

Multifactor models enable investors to zero in on risks that the investor has a comparative advantage in bearing and avoid the risks that the investor does not have comparative advantage in.

Multifactor models are superior to single factor models like CAPM when the underlying asset returns are better described by multifactor models.

ANALYSIS OF ACTIVE PORTFOLIO MANAGEMENT
Cross-Reference to CFA Institute Assigned Topic Review #54

Value Added by Active Management

value added = active return = active portfolio return – benchmark return

$$\text{active return} = \sum(\Delta w_i) \times (\text{return of security i})$$

Active return is composed of two parts: asset allocation return plus security selection return:

$$E(R_A) = \sum \Delta w_j E(R_{B,j}) + \sum w_{P,j} E(R_{A,j})$$

where:

$E(R_{A,j})$ = expected active return within asset class j = $E(R_{Pj}) - E(R_{Bj})$

Δw_j = active weight of security j = $w_{Pj} - w_{Bj}$

Sharpe Ratio and Information Ratio

$$\text{Sharpe ratio} = SR = \frac{R_P - R_F}{\sigma_P}$$

$$\text{Information ratio} = IR = \frac{R_P - R_B}{\sigma_{(R_P - R_B)}} = \frac{R_A}{\sigma_A} = \frac{\text{active return}}{\text{active risk}}$$

$$\text{unconstrained portfolio optimal active risk} = \sigma_A^* = \frac{IR}{SR_B}\sigma_B$$

The Sharpe ratio of a portfolio comprised of an optimal proportion of benchmark portfolio and active portfolio is $SR_P = \sqrt{SR_B^2 + IR_P^2}$.

Unlike the Sharpe ratio, the information ratio is altered by the addition of cash or use of leverage. For an unconstrained portfolio, the information ratio is unaffected by the aggressiveness of active weights.

The Fundamental Law of Active Portfolio Management

The three components of the information ratio are:

1. The information coefficient (measure of manager's skill).

2. The breadth (number of independent active bets).

3. The transfer coefficient (the degree of constraints on manager's active management).

$$IR = (TC)IC\sqrt{BR}$$

$$E(R_A) = (TC)IC\sqrt{BR}\sigma_A$$

For an unconstrained portfolio, TC = 1.

Selecting an Investment Manager and Choosing the Level of Active Portfolio Risk

An investor will always choose the active manager with the highest information ratio regardless of her risk aversion.

The investor will combine the active portfolio with the highest information ratio and the benchmark to create a portfolio with a suitable level of optimal risk based on their risk preferences.

Active Management Strategies and the Fundamental Law of Active Management

The information coefficient of a market timer = IC = 2(% correct) − 1.

The fundamental law can also be used to evaluate active sector rotation strategies.

Strengths and Limitations of the Fundamental Law of Active Management

While the fundamental law can be used for evaluating market timing, security selection, and sector rotation strategies, one has to be aware of its practical limitations.

The limitations of the fundamental law include bias in measurement of the ex-ante information coefficient and lack of true independence while measuring the breadth of an active strategy.

Economics and Investment Markets
Cross-Reference to CFA Institute Assigned Topic Review #55

Market Value of Assets

The value of any asset can be computed as present value of its expected future cash flows discounted at an appropriate risk-adjusted discount rate. Risky cash flows require the discount rate to be higher due to inclusion of a risk premium. Market prices reflect current expectations. Only changes in expectations cause a change in market price.

Short-Term Interest Rates

Interest rates are positively related to GDP growth rate and to the expected volatility in GDP growth due to a higher risk premium. When the economy is in recession, short-term policy rates tend to be low. Investor expectations about higher future GDP growth and inflation as the economy comes out of recession lead to higher longer-term rates. This leads to positive slope of the yield curve. Conversely, an inversely sloping yield curve is often considered a predictor of future recessions.

Yield Spreads Between Non-Inflation-Adjusted and Inflation-Indexed Bonds

Break-even inflation rate (BEI)

= yield on non-inflation-indexed bonds – yield on inflation-indexed bonds

BEI is comprised of two elements: expected inflation (π) and risk premium for uncertainty in inflation (θ).

Credit Spreads

Credit spreads tend to rise during times of economic downturns and shrink during expansions. When spread narrows, lower-rated bonds tend to outperform higher-rated bonds. Spreads for issuers in the consumer cyclical sector widen considerably during economic downturns compared to spreads for issuers in the consumer non-cyclical sector.

Phase of the Business Cycle and Earnings Growth Expectations

Cyclical industries (e.g., durable goods manufacturers and consumer discretionary) tend to be extremely sensitive to the business cycle; their earnings rise during economic expansions and fall during contractions. Non-cyclical, or defensive industries, tend to have relatively stable earnings.

Consumption-Hedging Properties of Equity and the Equity Risk Premium

Equities are generally cyclical; they have higher values during good times and have poor consumption hedging properties. Therefore, the risk premium on equities should be positive.

Economic Factors Affecting Investment in Commercial Real Estate

Commercial real estate has equity-like and bond-like characteristics. The valuation depends on the rental income stream, the quality of tenants, and the terminal value at the end of the lease term. The discount rate for commercial real estate includes a risk premium for uncertainty in terminal value and also for illiquidity.

THE PORTFOLIO MANAGEMENT PROCESS AND THE INVESTMENT POLICY STATEMENT
Cross-Reference to CFA Institute Assigned Topic Review #56

Steps of the Portfolio Management Process

There are three steps of the portfolio management process: (1) planning,

(2) execution, and (3) feedback. The *components of the planning phase* include:

- Analyzing objectives and constraints.
- Developing an investment policy statement.
- Determining the appropriate investment strategy.
- Selecting an appropriate asset allocation.

Investment Objectives

Risk objectives are those factors associated with an investor's willingness and ability to take risk. Combining willingness and ability to accept risk is termed *risk tolerance*. Risk aversion indicates an investor's inability and unwillingness to take risk.

Willingness to tolerate risk is determined by psychological factors (i.e., subjective factors). For example, clients might feel their portfolios are large or that they are better than others at interpreting market or firm information. Other people are just naturally "risk takers." When a client makes statements about risk tolerance, you should interpret the statements as indicators of willingness, not ability, to tolerate risk. Always consider what the client does.

The client's *ability to tolerate risk* is jointly determined by the size of the portfolio (not the client's perception of the size of the portfolio), the client's time horizon, and the client's spending (i.e., liquidity) needs.

Guidelines on ability to tolerate risk:
- As the size of the portfolio increases → ability increases (*positive* relationship).
- As the time horizon increases → ability increases (*positive* relationship).
- As liquidity needs increase → ability decreases (*negative* relationship).
- If willingness > ability → must reconcile the difference by educating client.
- If willingness < ability → must reconcile the difference by educating client.

Return objectives are classed as either desired return (as stated by the client) or required return (as determined by financial obligations). Return objectives should be consistent with the investor's risk objectives. The objectives should differentiate between real and nominal returns, and pre-tax and after-tax returns. The return objective should be considered from a *total return perspective* reflecting both income and capital gains.

Investment Constraints

Liquidity constraints relate to expected or unexpected cash flows needed in the future. The liquidity constraint is closely linked to the risk and return objectives because liquidity needs will influence the ability to take risk and reduce expected return objectives.

Time horizon constraints are associated with the time period(s) during which the portfolio is expected to generate returns. There is also a link between time horizon constraints and risk objectives: long time horizons increase the investor's ability to take risk (although not necessarily the willingness to take risk).

Tax constraints depend on how, when, and if portfolio returns of various types are taxed. Investment choices must be made with careful consideration of how a portfolio's returns will be taxed.

Legal and regulatory constraints mainly affect institutional investors. The Prudent Investor Rule is an example of a legal constraint facing trustees.

The investor's *unique circumstances* are investment constraints that do not fit neatly in any of the other four categories.

Figure 1: Investment Objectives of Individual and Institutional Investors

Investor	Return Requirement	Risk Tolerance
Individual investor	Depends on life cycle stage and financial position	Depends on life cycle stage and financial position
Defined benefit pension plan	Sufficient to fund pension liability while accounting for inflation	Depends on plan features, age of workforce, and funding status of plan
Defined contribution pension plan	Depends on life cycle stage of beneficiaries	Depends on risk tolerance of beneficiaries
Endowments and foundations	Sufficient to cover spending needs, expenses, and inflation	Generally average or above average
Life insurance companies	Function of policy holder reserve rates	Below average because of significant regulatory constraints
Non-life insurance companies	Function of policy pricing and financial strength	Below average because of significant regulatory constraints
Banks	Function of cost of funds	Depends on business model and financial strength

Investment Policy Statement (IPS)

The IPS is a formally written document providing guidelines for portfolio investment decision making. The IPS does the following:

- Provides guidance for current and possibly subsequent investment adviser decisions.
- Promotes long-term discipline in investment decision making.
- Protects against short-term shifts in strategy when either market conditions or portfolio performance cause panic or overconfidence.

There are several elements to a suitable IPS: a description of the client's situation; the purpose, as well as identification, of responsibilities; formal statements of objectives and constraints; schedule of portfolio performance and IPS review; asset allocation ranges; and guidance for rebalancing and adjustment activities are usually found in an appropriately generated IPS.

Strategic Asset Allocation

The three common approaches to investing are:

1. *Passive investment strategies,* which include indexing and buy-and-hold strategies.
2. *Active investment strategies,* which include managing for a positive alpha and investing according to a specific style or in a specific industry or sector.
3. *Semi-active, risk-controlled active, or enhanced active strategies,* which include index tilting, where the manager over- or under-weights certain sectors of the index based on capital market expectations.

The final strategic asset allocation across asset classes reflects the investment policy statement and capital market expectations.

Essential Exam Strategies

Game Plan

This chapter provides important guidance about *how* to pass the Level II CFA exam. These insights and techniques will help you successfully demonstrate your hard-earned knowledge on exam day.

On the Level II exam, you are expected to demonstrate a greater depth of understanding than on the Level I exam, so success at Level I is no guarantee of success at Level II.

There are some important differences between preparing for the Level II exam and the Level I exam. First, the question format will be different. The entire Level II exam will be in an item set format. Item sets are short cases, usually about one or two pages in length, followed by a series of six multiple choice questions on the material in the case. The morning and the afternoon sessions will include ten item sets each.

We begin by showing you some proven approaches to mastering the Level II CFA curriculum. Next, we will communicate a plan for the last week before the exam. We will offer important suggestions to make sure you are prepared on exam day—that you're not so flustered by the time you begin the exam that your performance is negatively affected. We will also spend some time discussing strategies for taking the exam and approaching individual questions.

The Practice Field

As you prepare for the CFA exam, try to focus on the exam itself. Don't add to your stress level by worrying about whether or not you'll pass or what might happen if you don't. Many of the tips we provide are proven exam-day stress reducers. Your grasp of the content, combined with our test-taking tips, should have you very well prepared for the exam. You will be ready for the questions, and you will be ready for the exam experience.

All of the faculty at Kaplan Schweser have earned the CFA charter and have extensive experience teaching the topics covered in the CFA curriculum. We know what you are experiencing, and we have witnessed thousands of candidates go through the process of earning the right to use the CFA designation. Now, we want to share with you the time-honored strategies that we have personally seen lead to success on the Level II exam.

There are two fundamentals for success on the Level II exam: focus on the big picture and know the main concepts.

The Big Picture

Focusing on the big picture means you should know something about as many concepts as possible. For example, many candidates are not comfortable with pension accounting, because it seems to them like a lot of adjustments that do not make a big difference in analyzing a stock. Our advice is to learn some of the basics for the exam. For example, learn the differences between IFRS and U.S. GAAP in recognizing pension expense in income statement versus OCI. By remembering some basic information on exam day, you will be able to narrow your answer choices on an item set. You probably won't get every question correct with only a basic grasp of the concept, but you can improve your odds on a multiple-choice question from 33% to 50% by eliminating one incorrect answer choice. Also, you will be better able to discriminate between relevant and irrelevant information in a question.

Another component of the big picture focus is studying as many topics as possible. It is a poor exam strategy to ignore significant pieces of the curriculum. Some candidates believe that as long as they know a few topics very well, they can bluff their way through the rest of the exam. These may be smart people, but their exam strategy isn't smart.

Know the Main Concepts

By knowing the main concepts, we mean identifying the "must know" Level II concepts. With the help of many experienced folks here at Kaplan Schweser, we have done some of that in the previous chapters of this book. These are the concepts that we think you have to know to be successful on the Level II exam. In any given year, some of these concepts might be omitted, but if you can answer every question on these concepts, you can dramatically increase your odds of passing the exam. Generally, the idea is to be correct on most of the questions on important concepts, and then rely on your "big picture" knowledge to get points on the remaining material.

Topic Weighting

In preparing for the exam, you must pay attention to the weights assigned to each topic in the curriculum. The topic weights are as follows:

Topic	Exam Weight
Ethical and Professional Standards	10–15%
Quantitative Methods	5–10%
Economics	5–10%
Financial Reporting and Analysis	15–20%
Corporate Finance	5–15%
Equity	15–25%
Alternative Investments	5–10%
Fixed Income	10–20%
Derivatives	5–15%
Portfolio Management	5–10%
Total	**100%**

Formulas

There are many areas where you will need a comprehensive grasp of the material. The big picture approach will help you master large parts of the curriculum, but there is material that will be tested in detail. However, at Level II, the emphasis shifts away from blindly memorizing formulas and then plugging numbers into them and grinding out an answer. Instead, you also need to know in which situations the formula can be applied appropriately and the assumptions that support it. Being able to work with formulas will be important to your exam day success, but don't focus on simply memorizing them.

RULE BOOK

At some point in your studies, we recommend that you take time to review the information in the "Candidate Resources" section of CFA Institute Web site (*www.cfainstitute.org*). Believe it or not, you will probably find this to be a nice break from accounting or derivatives! For example, be sure that you are able arrive on exam day with a *valid* (not expired) *international travel passport*. Select an approved calculator (TI BA II Plus or HP 12C) and learn how to use it. Read the Candidate Bulletins that are issued by CFA Institute in the months before the exam, and be aware of items you can and cannot take to the exam. CFA Institute strictly prohibits taking any of the following into the testing room:

- Food or drinks.
- Backpacks, briefcases, or luggage of any kind.
- Any study materials.
- Scratch paper or calculator manuals.
- Highlighters, rulers, or correction fluid (white-out).
- Cell phones or any personal electronics.

These policies *will* apply to *you*. Every year, many candidates have problems on exam day because they assume their case is a legitimate exception. There is no such thing. If you read the rules and follow them, you will reduce the potential for unexpected stress on exam day.

FINAL WARM-UPS

You should have a definite strategy for the last week before the exam. If possible, take at least some of the week off from work. You should save at least one practice exam (six hours) for this last week. To simulate the actual exam, avoid looking through or studying this exam until you are ready to sit down and take it for the first time. Take the exam early in the week, and time yourself. Then, use the results to determine where to focus your study efforts over the last few days. You should devote most of your time to areas where you performed poorly, but spend enough time on your stronger topics to keep them fresh in your mind and keep your confidence level up.

Visit the actual exam center sometime during the week before the exam. Determine how long it will take to get there on exam day and where you can park. Even if you are returning to the same site where you took the Level I exam, be sure nothing has changed. Locate a nearby lunch destination in the area. The fewer surprises and distractions on exam day, the better.

Expect problems on exam day. Be prepared for things like cold or hot rooms, noise, or long lines. There are likely to be some of these that you cannot control, but if you are prepared for them, your exam performance is less likely to be affected.

Avoid "binge" studying the evening before the exam. Relax and make a concerted effort to get a good night's sleep; tired candidates make silly mistakes on the CFA exam. You will miss easy points if you are not rested. This seems like a trite point, but it is difficult to overemphasize the importance of going into the exam well-rested.

CFA Institute Question Construction Guidelines

CFA Institute has released very specific guidelines it uses to develop multiple choice questions. We will review the most important issues, but refer to the Candidate Resources section of the CFA Institute Web site (*www.cfainstitute.org*) for more detailed information.

Construction of Multiple Choice Questions

Item set questions on the Level II CFA exam consist of a one- to two-page vignette, a stem (which can be a question, a statement, or a table), and three possible answers labeled A, B, and C. One of the three choices is the correct answer and the other two are incorrect.

The incorrect choices are carefully selected to be common errors made by candidates, so don't be lulled into a false sense of security just because your answer happens to show up among the choices.

Word Choice in Stems

According to CFA Institute, stems do not use the following terms:

- EXCEPT.
- TRUE.
- FALSE.

NOT is avoided whenever possible, although it's likely you'll see at least a few questions on the Level II exam that include NOT in the stem.

Many stems, however, do use qualifying words such as:

- *Most* likely.
- *Least* likely.
- *Best* described.
- *Most* appropriate.
- *Most* accurate.
- *Least* appropriate.
- *Least* accurate.

Questions that require a calculation, such that the choices are numerical choices (as in our example), will often use "closest to." If you've taken the right approach on the question, your answer will be very close to one of the choices, and not nearly as close to any of the others.

Notice that this is consistent with the idea that you should choose the "best" response among the three choices. It is possible, for example, that you could argue that two choices are "appropriate," but only one of them is "most appropriate." Don't spend your time creating unlikely scenarios where another choice might just be possible in some unusual circumstance.

CFA Institute does not use any of the following as answer choices:

- All of the above.
- None of the above.
- Cannot determine.
- Cannot calculate.
- Not enough information to determine.

How is an Item Set (Selected Response) Different From Level I Multiple Choice?

An item set is a short story, called a vignette, followed by a series of six questions. The Level II exam will consist of ten item sets in the morning, and ten item sets in the afternoon. According to CFA Institute, the vignette is usually about one and one-half pages in length, although some are more than two pages, and a few are less than one page. You will have 18 minutes for each item set (three minutes for each of the six questions), but remember that you must allow time to read and digest the information given. It is generally a good idea to skim through the vignette once, just enough to get the basic idea (without trying to memorize each detail), and then read the questions. As you answer each question, refer back to the vignette to verify your facts and be sure that they support the answer selected.

According to CFA Institute, 30–40% of the Level II questions will be quantitative, meaning that calculations will be required to determine the answer. The remaining questions will be qualitative, requiring knowledge of how to apply and interpret the concepts in the curriculum. Note that this can include the interpretation of numerical data that is provided for you. Don't expect the qualitative questions to be easier than the quantitative ones.

Answering a Multiple Choice Question in a Level II Item Set

Here are some tips to keep in mind as you work through item set questions:

- Do *not* judge the facts presented in the case. If part of the scenario seems unrealistic, do not twist the facts to fit your "real world" understanding of the topic. Accept the facts as given and answer the questions using the CFA curriculum.

- Read each question carefully! Watch for double negatives, like "All of the following are disadvantages except:" It is very important not to miss words by reading too quickly; for example, "most likely" instead of "least likely."

> *Professor's Note: One suggestion to keep "least likely" and "most likely" straight on the exam is to cross out "least likely" and put FALSE, and cross out "most likely" and put "TRUE." Always remember, though, that you are looking for the best answer.*

- Read *all* answer choices. Don't just stop when you get to one that sounds right; there may be a better choice.
- After you read each question, formulate your own answer before reading the answer choices. Anticipate what you expect the answer to be.
- On calculation problems, after you select an answer choice, pause for a moment and think about whether the answer makes sense. Is the sign (positive or negative) of your answer correct, or does the direction of change make sense?
- Do not look for patterns in a series of answers. Just because the last three questions all had "C" for an answer, do not expect that the next question must be "A." There is no reason to expect that CFA Institute has any preference as to how many questions have one letter answer or another.
- Be *very* sure that you mark your answer in the right place on the answer sheet. If you skip questions or do the topics out of order, be careful to check yourself. Mis-marking can be devastating if you do not catch it soon enough!
- Finally, *do not lose your confidence.* Nobody gets a perfect score on the CFA exam; it just does not happen. Remember, the passing score is less than 70%. That means you can answer more than 30% of questions (108 points) incorrectly and still pass. Even if you begin to struggle on a few questions (or even five or six in a row), do not lose your confidence.

What to Do With a Difficult Question in an Item Set

You will run into questions that give you trouble. You might not understand the question, you may think none of the answers make sense, or you may not know that concept. Here are some tips to follow if you find yourself facing a difficult question:

- If the question does not make sense, or if none of the answers look correct, reread the question to see if you missed something. If you are still unsure, mark an answer choice and move on.
- *Never leave an answer blank.* A blank answer has a maximum point value of zero. A randomly marked answer has an expected value of $0.33 \times 3 = 1.0$ point. You are not penalized for wrong answers.

Time Management: General Comments

Candidates who fail the CFA exam frequently cite time management as their biggest downfall. Here are some tips to help you manage your time wisely:

- Take at least one practice exam and time yourself. This will give you some indication of whether you will have problems on exam day.
- One way to alleviate time pressure is to bank a few minutes by doing an easy topic first. Select a topic with which you feel comfortable, and go there first.
- Have a lunch destination planned beforehand.

Exam Day Tips

Keep the following in mind going into your test:

- Check your passport to make sure it doesn't expire before exam day.
- Print your exam ticket from the CFA Institute website. Make sure your name appears on the ticket the same way as in your passport. Don't write anything on your exam ticket.
- Read the Testing Policies page on the CFA Institute website.
- Visit your test site before exam day to plan for travel time, parking, and lunch.
- Get plenty of sleep the night before; don't stay up cramming.
- Review the Code and Standards on the day before the exam.
- The exam room might be either too hot or too cold. Layer your clothing.
- Get to the testing site early, so you are not rushed. Expect a crowd at the larger sites.
- Don't unseal your exam packet until the proctor tells you to.
- Don't assume anything that is not given in the question.
- Don't jump to conclusions; read all three answer choices.
- Pace yourself. Don't rush excessively, but even more importantly, be sure not to get bogged down.
- If you run into an especially long or tough question, don't dwell on it. Take an educated guess and come back to it later if time permits.
- Fill in an answer for every question. There is no penalty for guessing; all that counts is the number of correct answers.
- Do not let your eyes wander around the room. Never look at or even give the appearance of looking at another candidate's paper.
- Put your pencil down immediately when the proctor calls time. Don't be that guy!

INDEX

A

abandonment options 71
ability to tolerate risk 175
absolute convergence 41
accounting income 72
accumulated postretirement benefit
    obligation (APBO) 57
acquisition forms 84
acquisition method 50
acquisitions 82
active investment strategies 177
active risk 169
adjusted beta 93
after-tax operating cash flow 68
agency relationship 81
amortization and deferral of gains or losses
    55
amortization of unrecognized prior service
    cost 55
analysis of variance (ANOVA) 14, 15
antitrust action 86
arbitrage opportunity 168
arbitrage pricing theory (APT) 168
asset purchase 83
asset purchase option 52
asymmetric information 75
at-risk equity investment 52
attitude of target management 84
autoregressive (AR) model 18
Autoregressive Conditional
    Heteroskedasticity (ARCH) 23

B

backwardation 131, 154
bargaining power of buyers 94
bargaining power of suppliers 95
bear hug 84
beta estimation 93
binomial option pricing model (OPM) 156
Black-Scholes-Merton (BSM) model 158

bootstrapping 82
bottom-up analysis 96
breadth 172

C

calculating the translation gain or loss 60
call option 157
capital budgeting 68
capital rationing 71
capital structure 73, 75, 76
caplets 158
carried interest 129
cash-and-carry arbitrage 153
cash divestitures 89
cash flow estimation 68, 69
cash offer 89
CFA Institute Research Objectivity
    Standards 8
chain rule of forecasting 18
choice of accounting method 51
claims valuation 73
classical growth theory 40
clawback 129
club convergence 41
Code of Ethics 1
coefficient instability 22
coefficient of determination 15
cointegration 22
collateral return 131
commercial real estate 174
commodity futures 130
comparable company analysis 87
comparable transaction analysis 87
compensation arrangements 6
competitive advantage 94
conditional convergence 41
confidence interval 16
confidentiality 5
conflicts of interest 7
conglomerate mergers 82
consolidation requirements 52

Index

Index

Notes

Notes